★ LEARN 18 TECHNIQUES ★ MAKE IT UNIQUE ★ 25 PROJECTS ★ PAINT IT ★ STAMP IT ★ DYE IT ★ HAVE FUN ★ GREAT FOR BEGINNERS ★ 9 NO-SEW PROJECTS ★

bend the rules
« WITH »
FABRIC

FUN SEWING PROJECTS WITH STENCILS, STAMPS,
DYE, PHOTO TRANSFERS, SILK SCREENING, AND MORE

★ **AMY KAROL** ★
Author of *Bend-the-Rules Sewing*

POTTER
CRAFT

NEW YORK

Copyright © 2009 by Amy Karol

Published in the United States by Potter Craft, an imprint of the Crown Publishing Group,
a division of Random House, Inc., New York.
www.crownpublishing.com
wwww.pottercraft.com

POTTER CRAFT and colophon is a registered trademark of Random House, Inc.

Library of Congress Cataloging-in-Publication Data

Karol, Amy.
 Bend the rules with fabric : fun sewing projects with stencils, stamps, dye, photo
transfers, silk screening, and more / Amy Karol.—1st ed.
     p.   cm.
   Includes index.
   ISBN 978-0-307-45183-5
   1. Textile painting.   2. Textile printing.   I. Title.
   TT851.K375 2009
   746.6—dc22

2008050343

Printed in China

Design by Amy Sly
Photography by Alexandra Grablewski
How-To Photography by Matt Wong
Tech Editing by Mariko Fujinaka
Cameo illustrations by Cut Arts

10 9 8 7 6 5 4 3 2 1

First Edition

FOR MY 3
DISHEVELED FAIRIES:

MAY YOU ALWAYS MAKE MESSES.

CONTENTS

PART I
HOW TO MAKE YOUR FABRIC MORE LIKE . . . YOU!

1 A CRASH COURSE IN MIXED MEDIA ON FABRIC

2 GETTING STARTED

PART II
FABRIC PLAY! THE PROJECTS AND METHODS

3 PAINT IT

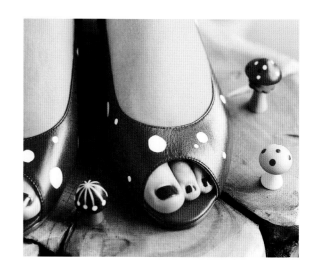

INTRODUCTION

As a kid, I loved altering my own clothes and fabrics. I was constantly drawing on shoes and T-shirts, embroidering my jeans, and adding bits of trim to all kinds of things. Later, in high school, I airbrushed T-shirts for my first paying craft gig. This was when I had my first sense that I was going to live a life filled with art and design—and a whole lot of messes.

There is something thrilling about marking up fabric. In my first book, *Bend-the-Rules Sewing*, I wrote about doing your own thing while learning to sew. Now it's time to have fun with your fabric. It's easier than ever to learn how to customize fabric—you don't have to take a college-level surface-design class. Nor do you need to break the bank buying supplies in vast quantities: Suppliers have made it easy to get materials, and much of what you need you already have around the house or can find at fabric or craft stores. Look in your kitchen! Stamping can be as simple and inexpensive as using a cut potato and some paint.

★ ★ ★

I have never really been able to navigate the distinction between art and craft for myself, and that's fine by me. Everything I make is a creative expression, whether or not it has a use. Not that I think art and craft are the same; they are not. But when I make things, I go with my gut. This applies to making anything, from a quilt to a painting. Granted, if I am working on a painting, the creative process is a little more abstract than if I am sewing a dress, but both come from the same place—the place of making something with my hands, something unique. When I sew a skirt I feel creative, but when I paint on fabric and *then* sew it into a skirt, I feel like an artist, and it feels good.

My hope is that you will have a blast marking up your own fabric, making some cool projects, and ultimately being able to see the hidden potential in an old piece of clothing or a new sewing project. You can use this book any way you like: as a workbook for your weekend projects, a how-to for printing T-shirts, a creative resource for making your own products to sell, a gateway to a new way of seeing old clothes in your closet, or a fun resource for making custom gifts for family and friends. Stay open minded, and make sure to tell people you made it yourself, okay? They will be impressed. And remember to have fun!

BRING IT ON!

This book is one part sewing, one part textile design, one part printing on fabric, and one part mixed media on fabric—there's a lot of information in here. I divided it up in an easy-to-follow format so you can learn most techniques without having to read a lot of text—perfect for you crafters who like to dive right in. Please have a peek through the entire book before you try a project, just so you know what's in here and can refer to it later.

You'll use a little bit of everything, from paint and dye to fusible webbing and even fabric sheets that run through a printer. You don't need a computer to do many of these projects, and some don't even require a sewing machine, but the more tools you have access to, the more fun you will have. Many projects use basic supplies from your own craft cupboard or are easily found at fabric or craft stores. Other projects require more supplies, so plan ahead before you embark on that new project at midnight.

Here's what you will find in this book:

A CRASH COURSE IN MIXED MEDIA ON FABRIC

This is a simplified overview of color theory, design, and tricks and tips to keep in mind when designing the look you want on fabric. There is also a section for some of you who claim you can't draw. Sure you can!

GETTING STARTED

Here you'll find a list of supplies followed by brief descriptions. Additional information can be found in the Resources (page 142), including where to buy. Next, there's a bit about what kind of materials to paint on, how to set up your space, what to do when it all goes bad, and other helpful information.

METHODS AND PROJECTS

This is the fun part. Covered first in each chapter are the methods—the nitty-gritty, nuts-and-bolts guides to different fabric-altering techniques. Then come the projects, which you can create at home. It's really important to read the methods section for the specific project you are making. Because many supplies come with instructions from the manufacturer, refer to those first. I also include tips from my own personal experience with these supplies. I have pretty much tried and ruined everything out there in researching this book, and it's been great fun! I can save you some time and money by explaining what to avoid and what works well.

TEMPLATES AND PATTERNS

A template is a design you transfer or trace. A pattern is a shape you copy, or transfer, and cut out. Also included are templates and patterns you can download as PDFs and print right at home, saving you a trip to the copy shop.

RESOURCES

There's a lot online, but many of the supplies are stocked at your local fabric shop and craft store. Shop local first, and if you can't find it, look to the Internet.

Drawn Bookcover page 108

PART I

HOW TO MAKE YOUR FABRIC MORE LIKE...YOU!

Here we begin with an overview of the basic elements of design and a refresher course on color theory. Then, in the glossary of materials, I go over the nitty-gritty for each material used in the projects and methods in Part II—such as what the heck it actually is and a recommended brand name, if applicable. (The Resources section on page 142 lists the places that sell this stuff.)

1

A CRASH COURSE IN MIXED MEDIA ON FABRIC

★ ★

Basic Design Elements

When designing your own projects or fabric patterns, it's helpful to break down specific design ideas. There are a lot of design elements out there; here are some that are particularly important when working on fabric.

SHAPE Enclose shapes with a line or make a block of color. They can be painted in or perhaps represented as a big appliqué.

LINE Make solid lines, dashed lines, dotted lines, and anything in between. On fabric, line can also be represented by thread.

TEXTURE This can be applied using different materials and methods, such as embroidery and drawing with thread.

COLOR There are several color elements in these projects: the color of the fabric, the color you can apply, and the color of thread. Some projects combine all three.

REPETITION This is a favorite element of mine for creating a pattern. A simple shape applied repeatedly to fabric is a quick and sophisticated way to make a strong graphic statement. A weak design can be strengthened immensely by repeating an element. It's like saying "I mean it!" instead of "I'm not sure."

GRADATION Mostly used in reference to watercolor on fabric or dyeing on fabric, this is when a color fades and is not uniformly one hue. A subtle element, it's great to apply when working with one color.

SCALE This can be big or little and everything in between. Imagine a polka-dot print on fabric. Now imagine that same print bigger. Then imagine it huge. The look changes significantly as the scale changes. A good rule of thumb is the larger the scale, the more contemporary a fabric tends to look. There are many exceptions, of course, but compare your typical calico print to a Marimekko print, and you can see what a difference scale can make.

BALANCE By *balance* I mean the balance of elements within a project—the perfect mix of bold and understated to make a project sing. Is paint enough, or does it need a little thread, too? This is all subjective—when a project looks "right" to you, it's balanced. Strive for that, and don't stop until you are satisfied.

Simple Color Theory, and How to Keep Track of Your Favorite Colors

There are university courses dedicated to this topic, but you just want to paint on your shoes! So here's the deal: When painting, dyeing, and altering fabric, you need to apply color with a bit more gusto. This is because fabric doesn't saturate as much as paper. Also, because we wear and use fabric, color subtleties can get lost in our movements, unlike the subtleties of a print behind glass hanging on a wall.

Look at the color wheel, and you can see how the colors relate side by side. Colors next to each other tend to be soothing together; these are *analogous* colors. Colors opposite each other are bold and tend to "pop" more; these are *complementary* colors. My favorite combination is split-complementary colors, which is similar to complementary colors but without the edge. For instance, instead of violet and

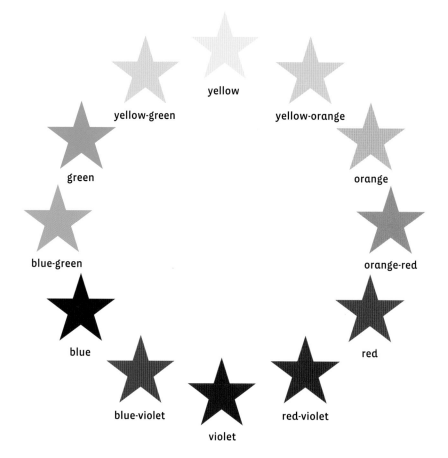

orange—true complementary colors—think light blue and coral, or sherbet orange and sage green. Split-complementary colors are not exactly opposite on the color wheel, but close to opposite.

Often when selecting colors or mixing paint, we get color amnesia. It's easy to use the same color combinations over and over again, but this can keep us in a creative rut. For a fun way to record and keep track of some of your favorite color combinations, go to a paint shop and grab a ton of paint swatches. Cut up the squares and glue them in different combinations into a sketchbook. It helps to overlap them slightly or have them touch, so you can really see the color relationships. Alternatively, use tiny slivers of colors as an accent, if you want less of that color in the combination. Use your favorite colors from catalogs or your closet to help select paint swatch colors. The next time you are mixing paint, pull out this sketchbook. All this color talk applies when selecting the paint for a project as well as the fabric to which you'll apply it.

"Help! I Can't Draw!"

I have heard this before. I usually hear it from friends who show me something they have drawn—and they can clearly draw! So first of all, you *can* draw. I know you can. But you might not be able to draw the way you *want* to. Fair enough. So let's instead focus on what you can draw and work with that. Anyone can draw circles, simple lines, blocks, grids, polka dots, squares, and rectangles (**A**–**D**, opposite). Just repeat these elements in a bold color a few times, and you will have a lovely design on fabric. I promise.

If painting or drawing freehand on fabric still makes you nervous, try projects that allow for more control.

» MIXING YOUR OWN COLORS «

I highly recommend getting comfortable with mixing your own dye and textile paint instead of buying bottles of each color. Mixing paint is one of my favorite things to do. I find it impossible to get the right color straight from a bottle unless I am going for a bright, saturated color like a classic apple red or kelly green. Plus, mixing your own colors will save you a lot of money. Buy the primaries—red, yellow, and blue. Then buy black, white, and a green, because green is a notoriously hard color to mix, especially bright green. Just start mixing, and you will get the hang of it. Mix with a small spatula or palette knife, not your brush.

Mixing dye can be experimental and hard to predict, but also a lot of fun. Making an entire spectrum of colors with just the three primaries is so satisfying. You can learn a ton about color this way. I highly recommend *Dyeing to Quilt: Quick, Direct Dye Methods for Quilt Makers*, by Joyce Mori and Cynthia Myerberg, to learn about small-batch dyeing and mixing your own colors. You won't believe how fun and easy it is to create your own colors. Some supplies used in the Dye It chapter (page 78), such as Dye-Na-Flow or Setacolor® Transparent Colors, are not dyes, exactly—they are paints that mix like dyes. Imagine mixing watercolors, for instance.

Some things to keep in mind when working with fabric and mixing paint and dyes:

- Paint is applied to the surface of fabric—it lays on top. So it will often deliver a brighter color than dye because it covers the fibers.
- Paint is pretty obvious to mix—for a darker color, add black or brown, and for a lighter color, add white. Dye is different, however. When dye is applied to fabric, it colors the fibers and becomes part of them. This results in a different type of coverage, usually one that is not as even. To mix dye, add more pigment to get a deeper hue, and add water to achieve a lighter hue. There is no white dye.
- Dye is transparent; you will be able to see what's underneath it (which is why dyeing over stains doesn't work). Paint is usually opaque, though transparent paints are available. When dyeing, white fabric acts as white paint would when mixing colors. This means you never know what a color looks like *until it's actually on the fabric.*

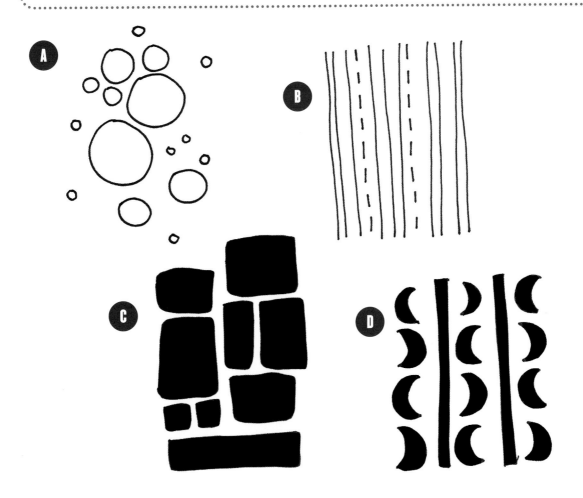

Fabric printer sheets, for instance, allow you to see exactly what you are doing before you print onto fabric. If you just want to focus on the process and not get all stressed out about drawing and painting from your own head, try using rubber stamps, copyright-free images, or printing your own photographs directly onto your fabric.

Start keeping a sketchbook and try to draw a little bit every day. If you doodle a lot, take a moment to really look at your doodles and imagine what they would look like blown up. Make enlargements way bigger than you would think to try. Pretty cool, huh? You have a fabric pattern right there. Make several copies and play around—color them in, change the scale, add thick lines and thin lines—then scan into a computer, and print onto your fabric. Or even burn a screen of your design. See, you can *totally* draw.

» WHAT IS A FABRIC REPEAT, AND DO I NEED TO THINK ABOUT IT? «

A fabric repeat is the measurement of a complete pattern on a fabric before it is repeated. Unless it's a stripe, this is denoted by its height and width measurement. Grab a patterned fabric, and with a ruler measure how wide and how high the pattern is before it starts again. This measurement is the repeat. Stripes have only one measurement, because a true stripe pattern runs in just one direction.

So, do you have to consider the pattern repeat when printing on fabric? Well, I love thinking about it, but you can skip it if it bores you. Here's the thing about the fabric repeat: If you print on fabric at home on your computer or use the silk-screening method, the concept will come up, so it's good to know about it ahead of time. Keep in mind that if you design fabric, the repeat should fit the scale of your project. So, if you are working on a pattern to print onto fabric from your printer, and you are using 8½" x 11" (21.5 x 28cm) sheets, you might design a pattern with a small repeat so you can see the design across the sheet a few times. When silk-screening, you can use this same 8½" x 11" (21.5 x 28cm) size and make it one full repeat, so that the pattern extends over a larger piece of fabric. This is a much larger repeat—but both use the same original pattern. If you bring this same pattern to a third-party printer at a copy shop, you probably can design using a much larger repeat because the fabric they can print on is so much wider.

If a fabric pattern has a large repeat, often the scale is also big, but not always. Scale and repeat are different. A small print may have enough variation for it to have a large repeat, even though the pattern itself is small. Imagine a kids' novelty print of the alphabet. The letters are small, but the repeat is big because it has to include all of the letters before it can repeat again. So, if you are interested, it's a good concept to know and be able to consider when designing fabric.

Copyright Issues

Using copyrighted images without permission is illegal. Ask permission before printing them onto fabric, or make it even easier for yourself—use only your own original artwork or images from a copyright-free source. There are hundreds of copyright-free image books and DVDs out there. Make sure to read the terms of use, especially if you plan to make items to sell.

Are you loving what you just drew and applied to your own fabric? Awesome! Consider copyrighting the pattern to protect your work at www.copyright.gov.

2

GETTING STARTED

Here is all the info you need to get started, including a comprehensive glossary of supplies with definitions and descriptions of their use in this book, ideas for types of fabric to apply paint, dye, thread, or images to, and tips on setting up your art space.

★   ★

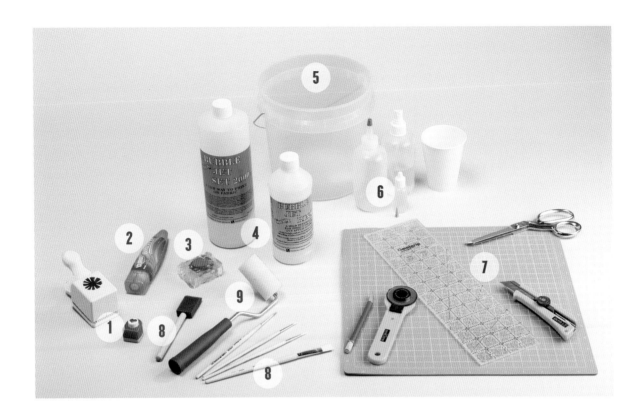

Glossary of Materials

(See the Resources section, page 142, for additional info and where to buy.)

Here's a glossary of some of the materials you'll need to start having some fun. Some of these items you will already have on hand, while others are totally obscure and you will have no idea what they are. Each project lists the necessary materials. Please refer to this glossary for a better description of a specific material.

General note of utmost importance: Never, ever reuse these supplies in the kitchen or for food. You can use clean food tools/containers for dyeing containers and paint, but afterward they should only be used for crafts. Label the dye container accordingly to make sure no one packs soup in it for lunch. Bad news!

1 CRAFT PUNCH Allows you to make stencils with a punch with no drawing or cutting necessary. Available in various sizes and shapes—hearts, butterflies, and so on (shown: sunburst, heart). The bigger the better.

2 BLEACH PEN Sold in the laundry/cleaning department of grocery stores, these can be used on fabric to make a faded line, creating a batik-like effect.

3 ACRYLIC BLOCKS For mounting foam stamps onto. Wood also works, but being able to see through the block while you stamp is extra handy.

4 BUBBLE JET SET 2000® AND RINSE Presoak fabric in this solution to make your own fabric sheets to send through your printer.

5 DYEING CONTAINERS Think yogurt containers, plastic cups, buckets—you get the idea. If you are dyeing small amounts of fabric, you can use plastic cups; otherwise you might want a bigger size. Collect things from your recycling bin. For larger dyeing amounts, plastic bins work nicely.

6 PLASTIC BOTTLES In various sizes with a variety of tips. These are great for applying paints. Buy metal tips to apply a thin line of paint or dye. They come in .05-, .07-, and .09-mm widths and fit in the tip of a $\frac{1}{2}$-oz (14ml) squeeze bottle top. These can be time-consuming to clean when changing colors, so have more than one on hand.

7 CUTTING SUPPLIES Craft knives for cutting stencils, and scissors for cutting both fabric and paper—ideally not the same pair. Rotary cutters, cutting mats, rulers, and straightedges are helpful as well (from bottom left: light-duty craft knife, rotary cutter, straightedge, heavy-duty craft knife, scissors, all on self-healing cutting mat).

8 BRUSHES It's good to have an assortment of round, flat, and foam brushes in various sizes. Don't get cheap ones, or the hairs will come off in your paint, which will make you crazy.

9 PAINT BRAYER This little roller is helpful for applying paint to foam and stamps.

10 IRON-ON TRANSFER MATERIAL This thin film is backed with paper. You send it through a printer and then iron on the transfer. This creates a mirror image of the original artwork on your fabric. It's also available in an opaque version, which is ironed face up on your fabric. Designed for black fabric, it is 100-percent opaque and has a plastic feel.

11 WATER-BASED RESIST I use a water-soluble resist in these projects. It's a thin paint that that can act as a barrier or mask when dyeing fabric—like wax does when making batik.

12 FREEZER PAPER Not waxed paper, but similar—it has a thin coat of plastic on the back, making it perfect for all kinds of surface design techniques. See the Freezer Paper sidebar on page 37 for more info about this amazing material.

13 ERASER CARVING BLOCKS These are not actually erasers, but blocks made out of an eraser-type material meant for carving.

14 IRON Used for adhering iron-on materials, heat-setting, and pressing seams open.

15 IRON-ON FUSIBLE GLUE This adhesive-backed fusible web, such as HeatnBond®, can be ironed onto fabric, then bonded to another fabric— perfect for applying patches and machine-stitched appliqué.

16 PHOTOEZ® A very handy alternative to traditional silk screening. A Print Gocco®–like screen coated with a material that allows you to burn a screen image without photo emulsion or drawing fluid.

17 FOAM This material can be cut to make your own stamps (it comes with a sticky back for easy mounting). Moldable foam stamps can be indented with objects, which is sometimes referred to as embossing. Mount to wood or acrylic blocks for easy stamping.

18 FABRIC PHOTO PAPER Paper-backed fabric that goes through your printer. This can be purchased for inkjet/laser printers and copiers.

19 FABRIC INK STAMP PAD When heat-set on fabric, this ink will not come off when the garment is washed.

20 TAPE Double-stick, clear, and packing tape are all useful to have at the ready.

21 LINO CUTTER This handy cutter with a U-shaped tip is perfect for carving your own rubber stamps.

22 FABRIC PAINTS There are a ton of different types available. Some are best for dark fabrics, some for light fabrics, and you can even get some with glitter. You get what you pay for, so if your item will be frequently laundered, it's best to get a high-quality fabric paint.

23 PAPER TOWELS/SCRAP PAPER Some supplies, like glitter and metallic paint, should really be kept away from all other things, so a paper towel for cleanup is nice because then it gets thrown away. Rags also work. Scrap paper is important to have handy for laying down brushes or anything else wet.

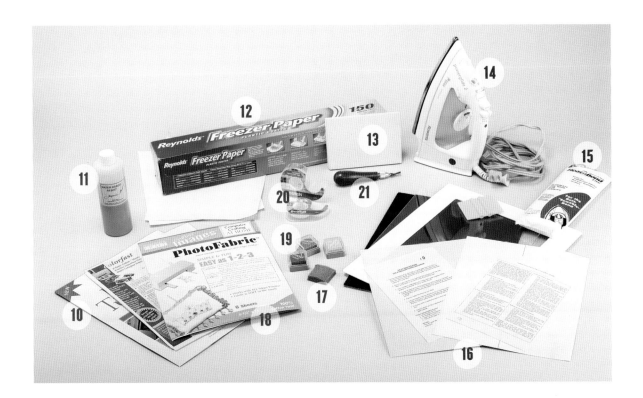

24 SODA ASH A chemical dissolved in water to prepare fabric for textile dye.

25 SYNTHRAPOL® A liquid soap used to wash out fabric dye.

26 SULKY® SPRAY KK 2000 TEMPORARY SPRAY ADHESIVE This nontoxic temporary spray glue is the perfect thing to keep materials in place on fabric for a short amount of time.

27 VINYL OR LATEX GLOVES Protect your hands when dyeing. Latex ones are available, or buy vinyl if you have latex allergies.

28 SILK-SCREEN INK FOR TEXTILES To use with PhotoEZ when printing on fabric.

29 RUBBER STAMPS From craft stores or your personal stash. A set of the complete alphabet is very handy.

30 PALETTES For mixing paints—paper plates, lids of plastic containers, and small ceramic dishes all work equally well.

31 TEXTILE DYES Procion dyes, Jacquard® Dye-Na-Flow, and iDye® are all used in these projects. There are other kinds available, but these create the most vibrant colors. Always use dye made for your fabric type—dyes for cotton won't work on synthetic fabrics.

32 RAGS Anything you don't mind getting permanently stained—old clothes and cloth diapers are great.

33 PALETTE KNIFE Use this tool, not a brush, to mix your paints. It will save your brush bristles and makes for easier cleanup.

34 PENS/MARKERS FOR TRANSFERRING PATTERNS AND DESIGN A water-soluble pen, chalk pencil, vanishing pen, and transfer pencil are perfect for transferring designs from this book and from your own sketchbook. A chalk pencil will work better on dark fabrics, while a water-soluble pen or vanishing pen works well with light fabrics.

35 MASKS/RESPIRATOR Dust masks are highly recommended when using dye powders.

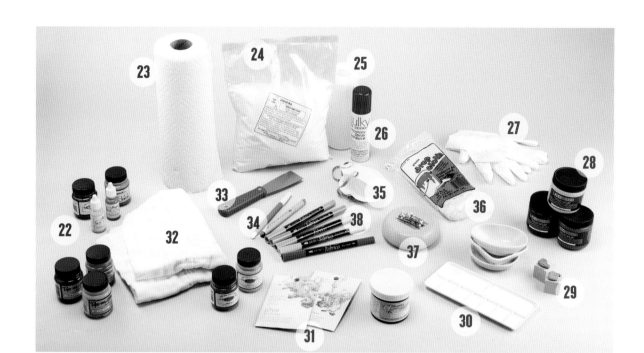

36 PLASTIC DROP CLOTH Protects your table or padded work surface. You can find these at painting supply shops—just cut them to size.

37 T-PINS OR LARGE PINS WITH HEADS For stretching/securing the fabric onto your padded work surface.

38 PENS/MARKERS For sketching and marking directly onto fabric; there are several brands available. For fine black lines, I like Pigma® Micron® by Sakura, and for colored lines, Fabrico Dual Marker by Tsukineko®. Check the pen for heat-setting directions if applicable.

(The following supplies were not photographed:)

39 APRON/SMOCK This will get very stained, so don't use your favorite. A pair of old jeans and a sweatshirt just for crafting is good, too—fabric paint and dye does not wash out, so protect your clothes.

40 TRANSFER PAPER Use this nonwaxy paper to trace designs directly onto your fabric. The marks wash out, and the paper is easy to use.

41 LIGHTWEIGHT FUSIBLE INTERFACING FOR KNITS This iron-on material is great for stabilizing

knits when you want to use thread as an embellishment.

42 PADDED WORK SURFACE This is optional but worth it if you can swing it. A board wrapped in batting and then canvas is a wonderful surface to work on and pin your fabric to. An ironing board can be used in the same way.

43 COMPUTER With basic photo-editing software (not required but handy) and a word-processing program with very basic layout options.

44 PRINTER A full-color inkjet printer is more versatile for mixed-media crafts because it uses no heat, although a laser printer is fine for projects not involving heat. Most fabric transfer supplies are available for both inkjet and laser printers.

45 SCANNER If you want to use original artwork, and if you want to make copies without leaving the house, this is very handy to have.

46 SEWING MACHINE Use one that allows free-motion quilting by lowering the feed dogs and using a darning foot. Look in your sewing manual for more specific details.

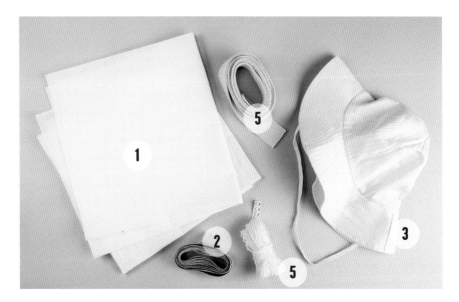

The Fabrics (and Other Things You Will Want to Customize)

Once you make a few of these projects, you will see fabric around the house in a whole new way. When looking for items to alter, from a store or your closet, the most important thing is the fabric content. Is it cotton, wool, silk, or polyester? Some dyes and paints work with all of these materials, some don't. Read the labels on the paint or dye before you start. Also, think about usage: Will the fabric need to be waterproof or laundered? If so, you need to be able to iron your item or throw it in the dryer to heat-set it.

1 PFD FABRIC PFD means "prepared for dyeing." It's fabric especially made to accept dye. It comes in a wide range of fabric types, from twills to cotton velours, silks, and even velvets. The fabric still needs to be prewashed, however.

2 FOUND FABRIC The sky is the limit here. Search your closet, Goodwill, and your fabric stash.

3 BLANK CLOTHING AND ACCESSORIES Clothing and items especially made for dyeing and painting. You can get dresses, T-shirts, handbags—even umbrellas—that are ready to paint on and dye.

4 SHOES Canvas, leather, and vinyl shoes can be painted on with textile paint—check your paint type first.

5 TRIMS Lace, thread, yarn, ribbons, and other notions can be dyed, stamped, and painted on. The easiest way to dye trims is to do so in small batches when dyeing clothes. Try to choose cotton trims, though there are dyes for synthetics as well.

》 A WORD ABOUT NOTETAKING 《

Most crafters and artists fall into two types: those who are natural notetakers, and those who are not. There is a third type, which is what I am: a notetaker and then a noteloser. It's horrible. I recommend getting a small notebook (wrapping it with the book cover project on page 108 would be perfect) and keeping it in your craft room for jotting down notes while you work. A sample page might have the date, the type of paint used on a project, the application method, and tips you might forget later. A handy template just for this purpose is on page 130. Print these out and put them into a three-ring binder. They are especially helpful for keeping track of your "recipes" when dyeing fabrics. You don't have to do this, but it can be fun and satisfying to see all of these pages filled with notes and fabric swatches when you are done. If this sounds tedious to you, then skip it, but at least have some scrap paper and a pen around, just in case.

ALTERING FABRIC VERSUS EXISTING CLOTHES

Altering existing clothing is thrilling and a wonderful way to extend the life of a garment. It also gives thrifted clothes a chance to shine. Most of these techniques can be used on existing clothes. If painting or dyeing existing clothes, first look at the fabric content and check to make sure your paint or dye is compatible. There are textile paints and dyes for nearly all fibers out there, so don't fret if your shirt isn't 100-percent cotton; just don't assume you can use one textile paint or dye for all of your ideas.

Also, many items need to be heat-set (see the Heat-Setting sidebar on page 39), but often a hot iron can damage the fibers before it sets the color. Look to see if you can use a clothes dryer in this case—it should specify in the manufacturer's directions for heat-setting. Altered items can hold up just fine with normal wear and tear, but will last longer if they are treated as delicates.

One huge bonus is that if you are painting or dyeing existing clothes, you don't need to know how to sew! I love sewing, as you know, but not everyone knows how, and not everyone wants to. I often alter existing clothes without picking up a needle or thread, because it's fun. No-sew projects are great for kids, parties (think a T-shirt-printing party), fundraisers, and group events of all sorts, so let your imagination run with it. There are so many blank, ready-to-dye items available, at craft stores and online, that you will have a blast.

Your Art Space

A craft room is a wonderful thing. If you have one, you can do most of these projects there, but if you don't, many can be done at a kitchen table, so don't fret. These projects use a variety of tools and materials. The sewing and computer work can be done wherever these tools are set up, but the painting and dyeing need a bit more care. Expect to run around a bit with these projects. For one project, you might need a sewing machine, an iron, a computer, and a sink—but that's part of the fun.

Dyeing typically needs to be done close to water, either in a washing machine, a large plastic tub, or plastic cups. If I dye in plastic cups on a table, I have to carefully transport these to a sink to dump them, so having a sink nearby is really helpful. If I am dyeing in a big tub, I place the tub in the sink so I don't have to lug a heavy, dye-filled tub around the house. Plastic tubs are my best friend for this type of mixed-media work. I can rinse in them, carry things in them (like cups of dye), and use them in my craft room when I am away from the sink but need water nearby. I toss in wet palettes, brushes, and rags while working. I keep a big tub on the floor by my chair, and when I need to remove a paint-filled brush or water cup from my work area, I just place them in the tub, paint and water and all. This way I never have to get up and wash as I go, and I can immediately lay out fabric and begin sewing knowing that all my wet items are off the table and can't be knocked over.

I use a large table for my surface-printing fabric projects, one that folds up and can be stored away when I am not using it. I make sure to have a comfortable chair. Good lighting, music, and supplies at my fingertips are important, as is a door that closes. Being interrupted while sewing is not usually a big deal, but being interrupted while painting or dyeing can be a disaster. Paint dries quickly and dyes are unpredictable, so I try to tackle these projects when I know I can work uninterrupted.

The dyes and paints I recommend can all be safely poured down the drain. If using supplies not mentioned, read the manufacturer's instructions to learn how to dispose of them. Consider placing a recycling bag in your area along with a garbage can. Many supplies and packaging can be recycled, and this is much easier if you have a dedicated box or bag to toss them into as you work.

I often drink water while I work, but I don't drink or eat anything when I work with dyes. When working in my art room, I drink from a thermos with a lid. This keeps particles out and serves as a visual reminder to keep me from accidentally drinking the paint water (I tend to get a little distracted while I work).

Prep

When you are ready to start a project, grab a few things to make it easier, especially if you are working with wet supplies. A spray bottle and rags and an empty tub to toss wet items into are all very helpful. Make sure all of your fabrics and items are prewashed. This is especially true for dyeing projects, because the dye won't cover evenly if there is anything on the fabric. Even if you are using blank or PFD ("prepared for dyeing") items, wash first.

A padded work surface can easily be made to place on your tabletop if you are screen printing and need a little cushioning. Just get some board (such as plywood) as big as your tabletop, and wrap it with batting and then canvas-weight cotton (you can also use cotton duck). Secure the fabrics on the back with a staple gun. I don't always work on a padded surface; it depends. I sometimes keep old towels on hand and then when I want to get messy, I duct tape these to my tabletop and paint right on top of them. When I am done, I take them off and wash them (by themselves). Experiment to see which work surface you like.

Plan B

Wrecked your fabric? Don't worry, there's probably a fix. Got all excited about a project and then found yourself staring at a completely ruined piece? Don't worry! It might still be okay. Read these tips to see if there's a solution. Also, before you start working or designing a project, it's good to have a plan B. The best backup plan is to always have more materials than you think you will need. Extra T-shirts, fabrics, and supplies can save the day. Sometimes this isn't possible, however, so here's a list to keep you from losing it:

★ Smudged paint lines and messy rubber-stamped images can be covered with homemade iron-on patches (page 106).

★ A painted image that looks horrible can be covered with another painted shape. Use a darker color.

★ A blotchy, uneven dye job can look intentional with a bleach pen design added to it (page 86).

★ Cut out and remove botched images on the fabric. Place a contrasting fabric behind the hole and hand-stitch the raw edges to the backing fabric for an arty reverse-appliqué look.

★ Try thread drawing (page 103) to cover up and distract from a less-than-perfect painting application.

Custom Baby Shirt page 118

PART II

FABRIC PLAY!
THE PROJECTS AND METHODS

3

PAINT IT
USING BRUSHES, SQUEEZE BOTTLES, AND STAMPS DIRECTLY ON FABRIC

★ ★

★　★　★

This part of the book is your reference section. It covers general instructions for the techniques that will prepare you for each project here or any you may dream up on your own. I have provided templates and patterns for you to recreate the artwork (page 120). Please refer to the Resources section (page 142) for more about each material discussed.

After each method is explained, its pros and cons are listed. These are helpful when deciding what methods to choose for your own projects. For example, let's say you want to make a gift for a friend—a painted pillow with a word on it. Since you are making only one and not reproducing it ten times, painting it would work great. However, should you later decide you want to include a silhouette as well as a word, you can paint the silhouette with a freezer-paper stencil and couch the word with yarn using the sewing machine. Look at you, fancy pants! You're employing two techniques in one project!

When using these ideas to design your own projects, the key to success is to choose the right method for your needs while keeping the original design, desired look, and end use in mind. This way you are working with your supplies, not against them. Here's another example: if you need multiples of a project—say, T-shirts for your new band—a silk screen with PhotoEZ will work great. If a slick look isn't your cup of tea, how about stamping the shirts with a hand-carved stamp? What if you want both a handmade look and the ability to make multiples? You can mix the two ideas and get a hand-carved stamp look on 200 T-shirts by screen-printing a hand-carved stamped image. Sound confusing? It's not—just read on and soon it will be like second nature. And if you do decide to take the hard road, who cares? Sometimes the best way to get your image onto fabric is by using what's on hand at 2 a.m., because all of the shops are closed and you are crazy anyway, staying up late crafting and all. As long as you are having fun, that's all that matters.

★　★　★

THE METHODS

FREEHAND PAINTING WITH A BRUSH

This is just what it sounds like—using textile paints and a brush to paint directly onto fabric, which is usually stabilized first. Depending on your design, this can be a line, filled-in flat color, or a textural/dry-brushed look. When using a brush on fabric, you will find yourself working harder to get a line than you would on paper. You have to load the brush with more paint and press down with more force. Testing and working on scraps is key.

There are many types of paint available for use on fabric. Some paints are perfect for dark fabrics, since they are very opaque, but that also means they dry stiffer and change the fabric's hand, or feel. Others are more all-purpose. Some work well on stretch fabrics, and some are a mix between textile paint and dye. Many textile paints work on multiple types of fabric, both natural fibers like cottons and linens and synthetics like polyesters. Check your bottle to be sure. Some can be used as an undercoat for applying glitter or foil, if you are feeling extra fancy. The list of materials for each project lists the type of textile paint needed. If you are going all renegade and doing your own thing, read the bottle before you bust it open and start painting. In most cases (especially if your item is going to be washed) you will need to heat-set these with an iron. See the Heat-Setting sidebar (page 39) for a bit on this.

MATERIALS

Fabric to paint onto

Fabric paint

Paintbrushes (rounds and flats of various sizes)

Palettes for paint mixing

Freezer paper (optional)

TEMPLATE *page 121*

1. Choose your fabric paint wisely. Each project lists the type used. If you decide to deviate from that and experiment, take note of what you used for next time, especially if you start mixing brands and types.

2. Stabilize your fabric by either ironing freezer paper to the reverse side of the fabric being painted (see page 37) or by stretching lightly and pinning to a padded surface, such as an ironing board or a padded work board.

3. Cut small scraps of your fabric and test the paint's viscosity on the samples before you start, adjusting the amount of water or paint needed. These scraps don't need to be stabilized—this step is just so you can get the texture right. Add water to the paint if you need it to be thinner, and test again.

4. Transfer your design (note: you may need to do this before you stabilize your fabric) as directed in the instructions for the project and paint over it, or just go for it and paint freehand. Sometimes I lightly draw my design with a water-soluble pen directly onto my fabric and then paint right over that. **A**

5 Let your paint dry. If you are impatient, use a hairdryer; otherwise, letting it sit overnight is best.

6 Remove the freezer paper from the back, and heat-set with an iron or in the dryer, according to the paint manufacturer's instructions. Heat-setting is no big deal—it really is just a simple ironing job. (See the Heat-Setting sidebar on page 39.)

WHY THIS METHOD WILL MAKE YOU HAPPY:

★ It's very spontaneous; almost no prep is needed.

★ Very few supplies are needed—just paint, fabric, and an iron.

★ It's very versatile. The paint can be applied to fabric, a finished garment, a pillow, shoes, etc.

WHY THIS METHOD MIGHT MAKE YOU SAD:

★ Some thicker paints can change the feel of the fabric.

★ Painting isn't the best method for detailed work or fine lines.

★ Painting can be intimidating, especially if you are new to painting in general.

★ Painting by hand is not the best choice for multiples (such as 20 handbags you're making to sell).

≫ STABILIZING YOUR FABRIC ≪

One thing that makes fabric painting different from painting on canvas is that the ground is different. The ground is how the surface is prepared. When you stretch a piece of canvas over a frame, the next step, before painting, is usually to gesso the canvas, filling the fibers completely with acrylic paint. With fabric we need to use some tricks to mimic this prep work, which is really important, as it keeps the fibers from shifting underneath your brush (or stamp or pen) when applying your medium. This is why the first step is to stabilize the fabric somehow. There are exceptions, of course, but for the most part, drawing, painting, and stamping on fabric is much easier when the fabric fibers are temporarily held in place. This is the key difference between having a good experience and a bad one in my book. So don't skip this step. (One exception is when working wet-on-wet for a watercolor effect. It's better to have unstabilized fabric to achieve this look.)

Stabilize your fabric by ironing a piece of freezer paper onto the back. To iron freezer paper onto your fabric, flip it to the wrong side, set your iron on medium to low heat, and place the freezer paper shiny side down on the fabric. Press with a dry iron (no steam) and lift up and press again, checking to see it's completely adhered. Remove it when the paint dries. This is the most stable method and the best for small projects. However, it would be crazy to use freezer paper over a huge area, so when working larger, pinning the fabric to a padded surface and stretching it taut works just as well. You can also cheat and work on a large piece of fabric but only use smaller areas for your design, stabilizing with freezer paper as needed right behind where you are going to apply your paint. See the Prep section for tips on how to make a padded work surface (page 25).

STAMPING ON FABRIC

Stamping is such a simple and pleasing way to get a design onto fabric. This is mark-making at its best. Think beyond the typical store-bought rubber stamps—carved lino blocks, carved erasers, leaves, fingerprints, cut vegetables, you name it—are all stamps. You can make, find, or buy your stamp, then apply paint to the stamp with a stamp pad, brayer, or brush, and you are good to go. You can use this method on both raw fabric and ready-made items, but the surface on which you stamp has to be as smooth as possible for a clear image. For fine, crisp lines, stabilizing your fabric first is key.

MATERIALS

Fabric to stamp onto (the finer the weave, the crisper the image will appear)

A stamp (either handmade or purchased)

Fabric ink stamp pad or fabric ink marker

Freezer paper (optional)

1 Stabilize your fabric with freezer paper (see page 37).

2 Ink your stamp using a fabric ink stamp pad. You can also use a fabric ink marker—ones with a brush tip work well—and brush the ink onto the stamp.

3 Stamp your fabric, pressing hard and rocking lightly back and forth. Sometimes a rigid surface is better than a soft one; practice on scraps first. **A**

4 Remove the freezer paper from the back, and heat-set with an iron. (Read the manufacturer's instructions on the stamp pad or marker.)

WHY THIS METHOD WILL MAKE YOU HAPPY:

★ This is a quick and easy way to add a fun look to fabrics. It's great for crafters who don't want to draw.

★ It's good for multiples.

WHY THIS METHOD MIGHT MAKE YOU SAD:

★ Image clarity is an issue. Getting a saturated shape or crisp lines is almost impossible. The image will looked hand-stamped and uneven. If this bothers you, try another image-transfer method, such as printing from your computer (Chapter 4, page 52).

CARVING YOUR OWN STAMPS

Also called *eraser carving*, this method allows you to create your own stamps easily by carving a soft material such as E-Z-Cut or an eraser. You can get pretty detailed with these stamps, depending on how much time you want to spend carving.

1 Draw your image on plain writing or printer paper using a regular pencil. Your final image will be the reverse of what you have drawn. So if using letters, reverse them and use a mirror to check your work.

2 Place your design, face down, on the top of a piece of E-Z-Cut, an eraser, or similar material, and rub with the back of a spoon to transfer the design. Remove the paper.

3 Start cutting using a craft knife. As the design gets more detailed, a lino cutter will be very helpful. **A**

4 Ink on a stamp pad or apply fabric paint with a brayer or brush (see the Applying Paint to Stamps sidebar on page 35 for tips). Stamp as you carve to see how your design is coming along. Test on a scrap of the fabric. When you are happy with the image, it's ready to use. **B**

5 Stabilize your fabric with freezer paper (see page 37).

6 Re-ink your carved stamp and stamp your fabric, pressing hard and rocking lightly back and forth. Sometimes a rigid surface is better than a soft one; practice on scraps first.

7 Remove the freezer paper from the back, and heat-set with an iron. (Read the manufacturer's instructions on the stamp pad or marker.)

WHY THIS METHOD WILL MAKE YOU HAPPY:

★ Carving your own stamps gives you complete control of the design. Plus it's cool.

★ Simple shapes make wonderful prints and are easy to cut (you can even just cut a potato in half). Stripes, circles, and squares stamped in a series is a great look and is super easy.

WHY THIS METHOD MIGHT MAKE YOU SAD:

★ All of the cool details might get lost when you actually stamp onto fabric—especially compared with stamping on paper. Simple is better here.

MATERIALS

Fabric to stamp onto

Carveable material (like E-Z-Cut or an eraser)

Craft knife

Lino cutter

Fabric ink stamp pad or fabric paint

Brush or brayer (for paint application)

Freezer paper (optional)

TEMPLATE *page 121*

STAMPING WITH FOAM

There are some super cool foam products out there for stamping. Foam is great for big blocky images. The foam holds more color, so you can get a saturated look easily when using fabric paint or a fabric ink pad. Fabric paint brushed or rolled onto the foam works better for bigger stamps. You can also press objects into the foam to make a relief pattern. Foam is easy to cut with scissors, and with a little double-stick tape it adheres perfectly to acrylic blocks, providing something to hold onto and a clear view of where you are stamping. Some foam sheets even come with a sticky back, so they are ready to mount as soon as you cut out your shape. Foam is probably my favorite material for stamping on fabric because I love how much paint it can hold.

MATERIALS

Fabric to stamp onto

Foam for stamping (see Resources, page 142)

Scissors or craft knife

Acrylic block or piece of wood

Double-stick tape (if needed)

Fabric ink stamp pad or fabric paint

Brush or brayer (for paint application)

Textile pen or dabber (optional)

Freezer paper (optional)

TEMPLATE *page 121*

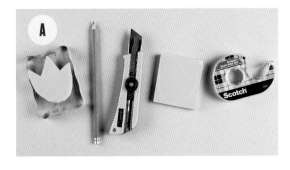

1 With a pencil, lightly draw your shape onto the foam. Use a really light hand here, because the pencil marks will indent the surface. If you are making simple shapes, like squares, don't bother drawing first—just cut.

2 Cut the foam with scissors or a craft knife just inside your line.

3 Mount the foam onto an acrylic block or piece of wood. If your foam does not have a sticky back, mount using double-stick tape. **A**

4 Stabilize your fabric with freezer paper (see page 37). Press the stamp onto a fabric ink pad or load paint onto the stamp with a brush or brayer, testing first on a scrap of fabric. You might need less paint than you think. Use a textile pen, a dabber (a sponge-y round stamp), or other materials to add detail if you want to. **B**

5 When dry, remove the freezer paper from the back, and heat-seat your design if needed (read the manufacturer's instructions for the paint or stamp pad). Wash your foam stamp well with soapy water.

WHY THIS METHOD WILL MAKE YOU HAPPY:

★ If you like both graphics and repeated images, this is your go-to method. You can cut several shapes and mount them to one block for an easy way to get a complicated repeat.

★ It's fast. You can sit down with very few supplies and get results right away.

- It's versatile. Because the foam holds more paint than a traditional rubber stamp, you can use this method for loosely woven fabrics. (And the stamps will work on paper, too! Bonus!)

- It works pretty well for multiples. It's more time-consuming compared with other processes, but because it's a stamp, the same look can be achieved over and over again.

- The stamps should last indefinitely.

WHY THIS METHOD MIGHT MAKE YOU SAD:

- It's not precise, the paint can smudge, and you will get uneven paint application, so it's truly a handmade look. If this bugs you, try a computer transfer method.

≫ APPLYING PAINT TO STAMPS AND CHOOSING FABRIC ≪

Ink and paint application can be tricky when stamping onto fabric. With paper, it's no big deal, but fabric fibers, no matter how tight the weave is, can create a less than clear or vibrant image. I like to apply fabric paint onto large stamps, especially foam ones, with a foam brush. You can drag the brush across the stamp, lifting off some paint or adding more, depending on your desired effect. You can also drag the brush across the stamp to create a cool textured look on the image. For store-bought stamps or carved stamps with lots of detail, I like to apply a fabric marker directly on the stamp instead of dipping the stamp in an ink pad. After you stamp the image (easier to do when the fabric has been stabilized with freezer paper), you can touch up the image with the same marker if you need to. I have had wonderful success with fabric ink stamp pads, but they dry up much faster than you would think. So if you love a color, buy a bottle of refill ink before you start your stamping project. The act of stamping onto the fabric is simple enough—a slight rocking motion seems to work best. Some images look best when you press really hard on a cushioned surface. Other images, especially ones with fine lines, need a more rigid surface. Foam stamps require less pressure than harder ones. Practice on scraps to see what will work best with your stamp.

WHICH FABRICS ARE IDEAL FOR STAMPING?

In a nutshell, the smoother your fabric, the clearer your stamped image will be. Coarse fabric with a low thread count, like canvas (or duck) and twill, will produce images that are hard to see, especially if the image has detailed lines. These fabrics are perfect candidates for foam stamps. A coarser fabric and a big, bold stamped shape is a perfect marriage. Poplin and high-quality cottons will produce much clearer images for use with detailed stamps. When stamping on found items, like canvas shoes, for example, remember that the ink or paint still needs to be heat-set, so don't forget about this step if your item needs to be washed or might get wet. (Read the manufacturer's instructions first, since not all paints require heat-setting.)

Now that you have such cool stamps, don't forget to stamp on paper, too! Or lampshades, journals, envelopes, wood . . . you get the idea. There are a ton of specialized inks out there for stamping, and it pays to get the right one so the image stays put.

DRAWING WITH PAINT AND A METAL TIP

The best way to describe this is to compare it to puff paint. Yeah, I know we all want to forget puff paint, but the application is very similar. Buy a small squeeze bottle, and swap the plastic tip for a small metal one. This allows you to draw with the paint in precise lines you could never achieve with a brush. The metal tips come in a few thicknesses. I never really pay attention to what size I use, as they all are quite thin, and that's all I need to know. Small bottles work best for this—it's easier to refill a small bottle than a big one. These bottles and tips are handy for all sorts of crafts, such as applying glue (great for fine glitter lines) and other materials. To keep the tip from clogging, slide a straight pin into it when you are done. These tips are small and easy to lose, so I tape them to the side of the bottle when I'm finished.

MATERIALS

Fabric to paint onto

Fabric paint

Freezer paper

Metal tip (0.5–0.9mm)

Small squeeze bottles (¹/₂ oz [14ml] works best; have one for each color)

Small funnel for transferring paint into squeeze bottles

TEMPLATE *page 122 (optional)*

1 Stabilize your fabric with freezer paper (see opposite page). For practice, you can trace a design by transferring the template from this example (see page 122) to your fabric before you draw with the paint. Or you can just do your own thing.

2 Either stick the metal tip directly onto the paint bottle or, if mixing your own color, fill a ¹/₂ oz (14ml) squeeze bottle with your paint using a small funnel. This can be messy and hard. Jacquard's ¹/₂ oz (14ml) textile paints are perfect for sticking a metal tip on, saving you this messy step.

3 On a scrap piece of fabric, draw with the bottle as if it were a pen. The lines will be thick or thin depending on how much you squeeze out and how fast you draw. You will also notice that the lines, especially thick ones, will stay wet for a long time. This is fine, unless your lines intersect—if you draw over these wet lines they will smear. So, if you want to draw lines over other lines, work in layers, drawing in one direction and allowing the paint to dry first. A blow dryer can help speed this up, but be careful: It's easy to get impatient and then smudge your lines. **A**

4 Allow to dry completely, remove the freezer paper from the back, and heat-set.

WHY THIS METHOD WILL MAKE YOU HAPPY:

★ This is how you get the look of a dark ink line on fabric, easy style.

WHY THIS METHOD MIGHT MAKE YOU SAD:

★ Wet lines can smear, so you have to plan ahead a little.

★ Sometimes if the paint is thick, the line will bead up and look a little like, well, puff paint. Use the very tip of a brush to flatten it out if this bothers you. And what's wrong with puff paint, anyway?

» FREEZER PAPER «

Oh freezer paper, how I love you! This one simple supply is perfect for so many crafting uses. First let's talk about what it is not: *It is not waxed paper*. That is a different kitchen item, and while waxed paper is much more commonly seen in the grocery store, it will not work for projects in this book. Freezer paper is similar, but it has a thin coating of plastic instead of wax on one side, making it stick better and melt more easily. Please don't try to make anything in this book with waxed paper; if it gets near your iron, you will have a horrible day.

So, where can you get freezer paper? Some grocery stores, in the same section as plastic wrap and waxed paper. Also look online. Reynolds is the brand most grocery stores carry, and they sell from their website, too. Also, since this is such a handy craft supply, there are precut 8½" x 11" (21.5 x 28cm) freezer-paper sheets made especially for fabric crafts. The paper and coating is slightly sturdy, making it especially nice for stencils and for stabilizing your fabric before feeding it through your inkjet printer. These precut sheets never jam in the printer, and they are also good for more than one use as stabilizers, so peel them off your fabric and use them again. The primary uses for freezer paper in this book are stenciling, stabilizing fabric to send it through your printer, and securing fibers when painting, printing, and drawing on them. Try these other handy uses as well:

★ Sewing pattern transferring: Trace patterns onto the freezer paper, cut out, and iron to your fabric—no pins or pattern transfer needed. After cutting around the freezer-paper pattern piece, peel off the freezer paper and keep it—it can be used again. This is especially wonderful for small pieces.

★ Appliqué ironing aid: When making small pieces to appliqué, cut out the piece in freezer paper and iron it to the wrong side of your fabric. Fold the fabric edge over the paper, making a clean edge, and iron. Remove the freezer paper before you stitch all the way around. Note: The lighter Reynolds freezer paper works best for this; precut sheets bond a little too strongly for easy removal.

FREEZER-PAPER STENCILING

A freezer-paper stencil is like any other type of stencil—using a mask (the freezer paper), you block out the area where you don't want the paint and then paint the negative area (what you have cut away). This is important to think about first, because the stencil needs to be the negative of where you want your paint to go. With the freezer paper method, crisp edges can be achieved that rival the best silk-screen method. However, you are only as good as your cutting skills. Also, this method is best with shapes that are primarily positive or negative. Think about the alphabet. The letter E is easy to cut, but the letter A is slightly harder because the middle of the A is free floating.

I have heard of people reusing freezer-paper stencils, but it sounds like a messy nightmare to me—I think of them as a great way of making a design, but good for one use only. But it is *so good*. The lines don't bleed under the stencil, which happens with most other stencil methods and can be maddening. This is probably my favorite way to make a unique image on fabric. Such simple materials for such a lovely result. This method uses freezer paper in two ways: as a stabilizer and as the stencil material. Please read the Freezer Paper sidebar (page 37) for more info about this magical material.

MATERIALS

Fabric to stencil onto

Fabric paint

Sponge brushes

Freezer paper

Craft knife

1 Stabilize your fabric with freezer paper (see page 37).

2 Prepare your image, and, using a piece of freezer paper as tracing paper, trace the design onto the dull side of the freezer paper. With a craft knife, cut out the area where you want the paint to go. Iron with the shiny side down, making sure the edges of the freezer paper adhere completely. Now, with tweezers, carefully insert any "positive" shapes you need to complete your design, like the middle shape in the letter P, for example, and iron them in place. **A**

3 Apply fabric paint to the negative areas of the design with a sponge brush. **B**

4 Let the design dry completely before removing the freezer paper—this usually means overnight. Resist the urge to remove it before the image is dry!

5 Remove the freezer-paper stencil from the inside, and heat-set according to your fabric paint directions. **C**

WHY THIS METHOD WILL MAKE YOU HAPPY:

★ This is the best and cheapest way to get an image onto fabric with silk-screen-like quality.

★ No smudging! The freezer-paper stencil, once ironed on, will not leak paint. It just won't.

WHY THIS METHOD MIGHT MAKE YOU SAD:

★ This takes a while. You have to hand-cut the freezer paper, and it's really hard to reuse.

★ If you don't like cutting with a craft knife, this might make you crazy. Change your blade often!

★ It's not great for images that have a lot of floating positive shapes (like the letter P).

★ Mass-production is tricky—freezer paper is not good for multiples.

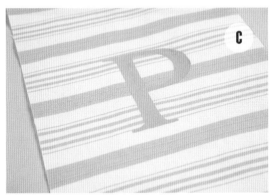

» HEAT-SETTING «

Don't fret over the idea of heat-setting. It's just a fancy way of saying "Iron it before it gets wet." So, when the paint, ink, dye, or whatever you are using is dry, you probably have to heat-set it before it can get wet again, especially before washing. If you don't it could bleed, smear, or eventually fade. Each product has different directions on how to do this, so read them. It's usually as simple as using a hot iron on the back side of the fabric for about 3 minutes. Sometimes you can heat-set in a clothes dryer, which is handy, especially when painting on shoes or lots of T-shirts. Blow-dryers can work, too. When trying a different method of heat-setting than what the manufacturer recommends, make sure to test first. Some textile paints don't even require heat-setting—bonus! If you are working with multiples, such as twenty-five T-shirts, heat-setting can take a long time. So allow for this when planning a project. If you are setting up a small shop, consider buying a heat press just for this purpose. They are not cheap, but might be worth it if you are making and selling lots of items that require this step.

THE PROJECTS

YOUR BLOUSE, ONLY COOLER

Raid your closet for the blouse or shirt that has never quite made you happy. This freezer-paper stencil project will add some spice to your shirt, and it requires no sewing. Just be warned—this is addictive.

MATERIALS

Blouse, T-shirt, or hoodie

Fabric paint suitable for your fabric (I like Jacquard Textile Colors)

Sponge brush

Freezer paper

Craft knife

TEMPLATES *page 133*

1 Read the Freezer-Paper Stenciling method (page 38). Trace the templates, or your own design, onto the dull side of the freezer paper. Cut out with a craft knife.

2 Iron the freezer-paper stencil with the cut-out design (not what you cut out) onto your shirt. Stabilize the fabric by ironing another piece of freezer paper to the inside of the shirt, right under the image. **A**

3 Paint with fabric paint using a sponge brush. Let dry at least 12 hours.

4 Carefully remove the freezer paper, and heat-set with an iron.

TIPS, HINTS, AND OTHER SUGGESTIONS

» Don't limit yourself to tops. Jeans, canvas bags, coats, and so on can all be altered this way. Just check two things first—the fabric content and if it can be heat-set.

» Want some sparkle? Try using a glittery fabric paint. There are tons of different fabric paints available in glitter and metallic colors, even glow in the dark! Try Glo Paint tubes (see Resources, page 142).

STAMPED BELT

This fun accessory can be made in no time and is a great way to add a little color to your jeans. Heavyweight cotton canvas strapping is printed with a foam stamp cut in a cute apple design and finished with a purchased plastic buckle. Stamping with fabric paint instead of a fabric ink pad helps achieve a clear image with super vibrant colors. And don't worry, the little green leaf is easy to do—it's just a dab of paint from a brush.

MATERIALS

1½ yards (137cm) 1½"- (3.8cm-) wide cotton canvas strapping (the length will vary; measure your waist circumference and add 8" [20.5cm])

Thick fabric paint like Jacquard Neopaque in red and green

Foam for stamping, like Sure Stamp Flexible Printing Plates (see Resources, page 142)

Craft knife or scissors

2" x 2" (5 x 5cm) acrylic or wood block

Acrylic buckle with 1¼" (3cm) opening (see Resources, page 142)

Double-stick tape (if necessary)

Paintbrush

Sewing machine (optional)

TEMPLATE *page 126*

1 Read the Stamping with Foam method (page 34). Trace the apple template onto the foam, cut it out, and adhere it to an acrylic or wood block. Use double-stick tape if the foam doesn't come with a sticky side.

2 Wrap the canvas strapping around your waist, ideally through the belt loops of your jeans. Mark where it's comfortable and add 8" (20.5cm). Cut the strapping.

3 Apply red fabric paint to the foam stamp using a paintbrush and stamp onto the strapping. Add green leaf details with a small brush. Just a dab makes a perfect leaf shape. Let dry and heat-set with an iron. **A**

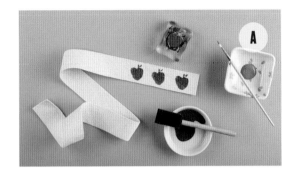

4 Attach the buckle by threading one end of the strapping through the middle bar. Turn the strapping raw edge over $^1/_4$" (6mm) and stitch onto the back of the belt about 3" (7.5 cm) past the middle bar. You will need the extra room to get your sewing machine foot past the buckle edge. Alternatively, you can hand-stitch this.

5 Try the belt on and thread the unfinished end through the buckle. If the length is right, hem the opposite end by turning over $^1/_4$" (6mm) twice and topstitching. If it's too long (remember that you will lose $^1/_2$" [13mm] when hemming), trim as necessary, then hem either by machine or by hand. **B**

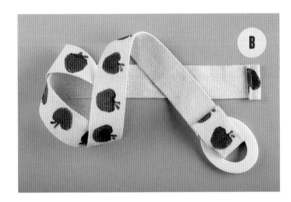

TIPS, HINTS, AND OTHER SUGGESTIONS

» When designing a stamp, keep the shapes simple. Add detail with a brush.

» Try to find strapping the same width as your buckle opening, but if the strapping is slightly wider, as it is here, that's fine. If you have a different-sized buckle, make sure it fits your strapping before you start.

» Although a little too flimsy for a belt, both lightweight and heavyweight cotton twill tape are wonderful to stamp on. Use them as trims and ribbon for gifts or embellishments on all sorts of projects.

DOTTED SHOES

Remember drawing on your shoes? I do. Mostly band names and whomever I had a crush on at the time. There is something so liberating about customizing shoes, especially when you use a design pattern that is pretty much no-fail—like this one. Just keep a wet rag at the ready and have a sense of humor.

MATERIALS

Shoes to paint on (the ones shown are leather)

Fabric paint suitable for heavyweight canvas or leather, such as Jacquard Neopaque (see Resources, page 142)

Small squeeze bottle with metal tip

Chalk fabric pencil

Small brush for touch up

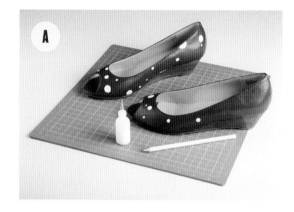

1 Read the Drawing with Paint and a Metal Tip method (page 36). Using a chalk fabric pencil, lightly mark where you want your dots to go.

2 Practice on a scrap of paper: Draw the dots with the metal tip, filling in by squeezing the paint. You will not be using the brush at all unless you need to spread the paint a bit. Paint the dots onto the shoes using the squeeze bottle and metal tip. **A**

3 Set the shoes up to dry and check often. If there is a lot of paint, it may drip while drying. Rotate as needed. Let dry overnight.

TIPS, HINTS, AND OTHER SUGGESTIONS

>> Using an irregular dot pattern is a safe bet. Because each dot and placement is one-of-a-kind, nothing will look like a mistake.

>> Less is more. You can always add more dots later.

>> Get a pair of thrifted shoes or a pair you already have that you aren't in love with to try this on first.

PAINTED TOILE

I loved coloring books when I was little. Using markers to fill in lovely pictures was the best. No worrying about drawing, no worrying about making a mess. This project will take you back to that nostalgic activity. Using toile (a fabric with a printed scene on it, traditionally in one color on a white background) makes it so easy; *toile* is short for Toile de Jouy, and it's the pattern on the fabric, not the weave. Your fabric shop can help you, or a quick search online can provide a ton of examples. Just fill in the fabric with a few colors and then pop it in a frame (either new or thrifted), and you have yourself a lovely piece of art. Don't feel guilty by how easy this is. There is no corresponding method to review here—just use the markers on the fabric like when you were a kid. You remember!

1 Take apart the frame and remove the glass if it's provided. Trace the frame backing board onto your toile with a water-soluble or vanishing pen. If your frame has no backing board, cut one out of foam core.

2 Cut out the toile piece, leaving 1" (2.5cm) on all sides for wrapping. Cut the flannel or batting to the same size.

3 Using the fabric markers, color in bits of the toile. You might want to try this on a test piece first. **A**

4 Layer the toile and the flannel on the backing, and wrap over the edge of the backing board or foam core and secure with tape.

5 I often frame these without glass. If using glass, clean and reinsert it, and place the toile-wrapped backing board into the frame—the fit should be tight. Secure with more tape if needed; often if the fit is tight enough it will stay without tape.

TIPS, HINTS, AND OTHER SUGGESTIONS

≫ Buy frames at thrift shops, garage sales, and discount stores, even if they have no backing board or glass.

≫ Use high-gloss spray paint to change the look of a frame. Imagine one bright color painted on several frame styles, all hung on a wall.

≫ This makes a lovely gift. A name or date could be added with some hand-stitching.

≫ Color in only a few small areas with marker for the most impact. Use the Painting with Dye method (page 83) if you want large areas filled in with color.

FINISHED SIZE
Small frame: 5¼" x 6¼" (13 x 16cm)

Large frame: 10½" x 12½" (26.5 x 32cm)

MATERIALS
Toile fabric, enough to fit in your frame, plus 1" (2.5cm) extra on all sides for wrapping

Fabric markers in various colors, such as Fabrico Dual Markers by Tsukineko

Picture frame (new or used)

Foam core, cut to fit your frame opening (if your frame came without a backing board)

Flannel, batting, or soft fabrics (the same size as your toile)

Water-soluble or vanishing pen

Clear tape, such as packing tape

(1) 1" x 2" (2.5 x 5cm) piece of Velcro®

ONE-OF-A-KIND CLUTCH

This rubber-stamped fabric looks detailed but actually stamps up quickly—it's one carved stamp that has four small designs. Stamping on a diagonal line makes this a little more unusual. This clutch can be tucked into a larger handbag or go out on its own when you are feeling minimal. It requires a small amount of fabric, so it's great for using up your stash.

. . . .

FINISHED SIZE

Clutch (with flap down): 8³/₈" x 4" (21 x 10cm)

Flap: 1¹/₄" (3cm) wide on the sides; 2" (5cm) wide at the middle

MATERIALS

Outside fabric (a light solid color works best for stamping): (1) 8¹/₂" x 11" (21.5 x 28cm) piece

Lining fabric: (1) 8¹/₂" x 11" (21.5 x 28cm) piece

(1) 8¹/₂" x 11" (21.5 x 28cm) piece lightweight fusible interfacing (you will trim this smaller)

Rubber stamp carving material

Craft knife/carving tools

Fabric ink stamp pad

Freezer paper

Chalk fabric pencil

Sewing machine

¹/₂" x 1" (13mm x 2.5cm) piece of Velcro

PATTERN *page 132*

TEMPLATE *page 133*

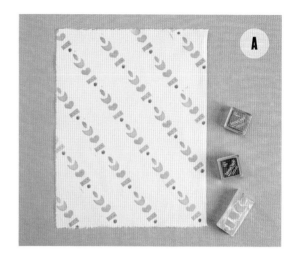

1 Read the Stamping on Fabric method (page 32) and the Carving Your Own Stamps method (page 33). Trace and transfer the rubber stamp template. Cut your stamps, making test prints as you go.

2 Prepare your outer fabric by stabilizing it with freezer paper (see page 37). Draw diagonal lines with a light chalk pencil 1" (2.5cm) apart. Ink your stamp and stamp onto your fabric. When dry, remove the freezer paper and heat-set. **A**

3 Using the pattern, cut out clutch outside, inside, and fusible interfacing. Iron interfacing to the wrong side of the inside piece.

4 Stitch Velcro® on inside fabric where indicated on pattern. **B**

5 Stack outside and inside pieces right sides together. Stitch around all edges, leaving an opening to turn right side out. Turn and press. Topstitch around all edges, folding the front up to make the clutch pocket while you sew. **C**

6 Pin Velcro® to front of clutch, aligning with the inside top piece. Stitch to front.

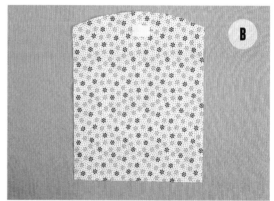

TIPS, HINTS, AND OTHER SUGGESTIONS

» You can skip the rubber stamping on this and just make the clutch.

» Because this project uses 8½" x 11" (21.5 x 28cm) fabric, it's perfect for use with Bubble Jet Set 2000 (see Resources, page 142) or fabric printer sheets instead of stamps.

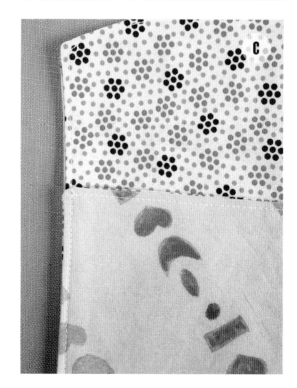

CUTIE UNDERWEAR AND CAMISOLE

Who doesn't need a cute set like this? This camisole and underwear set is embellished with freezer-paper-stenciled butterflies in metallic textile paint. The best part? All you need is your favorite craft punch; you can make this project in about five minutes. The longest part is waiting for them to dry. Plus, this is a no-drawing-or-cutting project! Amazing!

MATERIALS

Underwear and camisole set (100% cotton or a blend is best for fabric paint)

Fabric paint (glittery if you are feeling crazy, such as Lumiere by Jacquard or Jones Tones™ Glitter or Metallic Paint)

Freezer paper

Tools

Iron

Decorative craft punch (the bigger the better; see Resources, page 142)

1 Read the Freezer-Paper Stenciling method (page 38). Cut out several squares of freezer paper larger than your punch shape. Punch out the shape, maintaining at least ½" (13mm) of freezer paper around the punched-out shape.

2 Iron on the freezer paper negative shape. Stabilize the fabric with freezer paper on the back as well (see page 37). If the punch is small, this is not necessary, but do slide fabric or paper behind the painted area so the paint doesn't leak through to the back. **A**

3 Let dry at least 12 hours, then carefully remove the freezer paper. Heat-set with an iron.

TIPS, HINTS, AND OTHER SUGGESTIONS

» Craft-punched stencils can be used with any clothing item, of course. This is great for kids or anyone else who wants to avoid using a craft knife.

» Try making a set with the same craft punch but in different paint colors, one for each day of the week. This craft-punch stencil would look super cute on baby onesies as well.

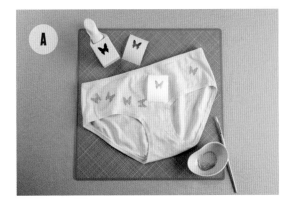

4

WE HAVE THE TECHNOLOGY
USING COMPUTERS, TRANSFERS, AND OTHER MIXED MEDIA ON FABRIC

★ ★

You don't need a computer to customize your projects, but it sure adds to the fun. A computer, printer, and—even better—a scanner open up a whole world of possibilities. No computer? Don't fret. Many templates used in this chapter can be sent through a color copier at your local copy shop. There are various ways to get the same result. For instance, if you have a scanner, you can scan the Templates and Patterns (page 120) or original or copyright-free designs directly into your computer and print them right onto your fabric sheets at home. If you don't have a printer or a scanner, you can take this book (or anything you want to transfer) to the copy shop and copy the image you need directly onto fabric sheets (or iron-on sheets) designed for copiers. Even easier, download the PDF templates available for some projects (at amykarol.com), so you can skip the copy shop altogether. If PDFs are available for a project, it will be noted in the Templates section for that project. When using the fabric and transfer sheets at home or in a copier, read the directions first so you don't get kicked out of a copy shop or have to explain to your friend why there is fabric jammed in her printer, okay?

But forget about the computer when you are designing your own art to print onto fabric. Even though you might use a computer for some of these techniques, that doesn't mean the *images* have to look digitally created. So many examples of uses for printed fabric sheets involve photos, which is great, but that doesn't even skim the surface of what you can do. For example, you can paint a real watercolor onto paper, scan it, and then print it onto fabric. Wow! You now have the look of a watercolor (a very tricky thing to do directly on fabric) printed onto your fabric from your computer. Same goes with drawing, painting—all of that. The computer is just a tool.

PRINTING IMAGES ONTO FABRIC SHEETS

There are many options out there, but the easiest way to print images onto fabric is to use sheets designed for your printer (or copier) that have fabric on one side. They are treated to take the ink and, in most cases, are permanent and can hold up to being laundered. They come in different fabric types, are usually only white or cream, and can be quite stiff. Several brands make them, and they can be found at most craft and fabric stores. Some things to keep in mind: Not all brands are waterproof/washable, so don't assume they are; read the fine print and care instructions carefully, making sure to check the type of fabric used (a twill is very different from a cotton poplin) and make sure to purchase sheets compatible with your printer—sheets are available for inkjet printers, laser printers, or copiers, and they are *not* interchangeable. Keep in mind when designing that the sheets are typically the size of a standard piece of paper, 8½" x 11" (21.5 x 28cm), but for longer lengths this material is also available on a roll.

MATERIALS
Fabric sheets for your printer or copier
Digital artwork or images
Printer

TEMPLATE *page 124*

1 Be sure to keep the packaging for the printer sheets you bought. Read the manufacturer's instructions. Prepare your image to print or copy. This might mean scanning a photo, uploading artwork, or scanning a pattern or template from this book (the template for the design used in this example is on page 124).

2 Always test-print on a page of plain paper first. If it looks good, load your fabric sheet and print.

3 If you are printing more than one sheet for a project, *wait*. Do not print on a second sheet until you go through all of the steps for the first. Once the ink is dry, proceed to the next step in the manufacturer's instructions. **A**

4 If it all works well, finish with your remaining sheets. I say all this because I once could not, no matter what I tried, remove the paper backing after I had printed all my sheets. I wasted time, money, and ink, and I was so bummed—so test first.

WHY THIS METHOD WILL MAKE YOU HAPPY:

★ It's very fast; almost no prep is needed.

★ Very few supplies are needed if you already have a computer and a printer (and scanner if you need it).

★ Because it's ink on fabric, there is no plastic-y feel to the printed image.

★ The technique is good for multiples (if you are willing to pay for the sheets).

★ You'll get almost perfect execution once you test (no paint to smear).

WHY THIS METHOD MIGHT MAKE YOU SAD:

★ The sheets can be expensive.

★ The product comes in very limited fabric choices that often feel stiff and un-fabric-like.

★ It's not archival. Even if it says acid free, your printer inks may not be, and these fabrics will suffer from UV damage and will fade. They just will, regardless of what any packaging says.

CREATING YOUR OWN FABRIC SHEETS

Bubble Jet Set 2000 (see Resources, page 142) is a liquid solution that enables you to make your own fabric printer sheets. That's very cool, and let me tell you why. You can use whatever fabric you want, as long as it is 100-percent cotton or silk. You can save a ton of money. The fabric feels better than premade fabric sheets and is much easier to work with. You also can use colored fabric. There are a few more steps and a bit of trial and error involved, but if you want to make a lot of images on fabric using your printer at home, Bubble Jet Set 2000 might be your ticket. Having said that—test, test, test. Here's where the headaches can happen. If the ink doesn't look right, it is because inkjet inks are mixed for paper, not fabric, so you might have to change your expectations about color and alter your images accordingly. Also, fabric can get jammed in your printer. The simple fix for this is to use purchased precut freezer-paper sheets to stabilize your fabric (not the freezer paper you get in the grocery store). The sheets can be reused several times, so don't toss them.

MATERIALS

Fabric to print onto

Digital artwork or images

Bubble Jet Set 2000 solution and optional rinse

8½" x 11" (21.5 x 28cm) precut freezer-paper sheets (see Resources, page 142)

Plastic tub for soaking and washing, at least 9" x 12" (23 x 30.5cm)

Printer

TEMPLATES *pages 127–128 (optional)*

1 Read the manufacturer's instructions to prepare the solution. There is quite a bit of info on the bottle and online. Think of this as a fun product to experiment with. It's not an exact science. Below is the process in a nutshell, but please follow the manufacturer's instructions.

2 Cut your fabric to 8½" x 10¾" (21.5 x 27cm), a bit smaller than the standard 8½" x 11" (21.5 x 28cm) size for fabric sheets. Soak the fabric in the Bubble Jet Set 2000 solution. Let it air dry.

3 Iron your 8½" x 11" (21.5 x 28cm) freezer paper, shiny side down, to the back side of your fabric. There should be a ¼" (6mm) strip of exposed freezer paper for the printer to grab—load this end first. If it grabs the fabric first, it will jam the printer. Trust me. Now, prepare your image, either by scanning your artwork, using an existing image on your computer, or using the template for the design used in this example. Print a test on regular paper first. If it looks good, load your freezer-paper-backed fabric into your printer, making sure the ink will be printed on the fabric side (which side is up varies depending on your printer), and print.

4 Let the ink dry (read the manufacturer's instructions). Peel off the freezer paper. Save that freezer-paper sheet! You can reuse it.

5 Once dry, rinse the printed sheet. Again, read the instructions on the bottle—there is an optional product recommended as an after-rinse.

6 Let dry (you can blow-dry) and then press with an iron and pressing cloth to heat-set. **A**

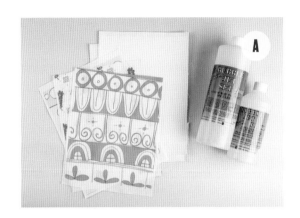

WHY THIS METHOD WILL MAKE YOU HAPPY:

⭐ It's much less expensive than buying packs of fabric sheets.

⭐ Printing yourself allows for many more fabric choices than what's typically available in the packaged fabric printer sheets.

⭐ You'll get almost perfect execution once you test (no paint to smear).

WHY THIS METHOD MIGHT MAKE YOU SAD:

⭐ It's not available for copiers, only for inkjet printers.

⭐ It requires more prep work than the ready-to-print fabric sheets.

⭐ The instructions on the bottle can seem intimidating.

⭐ It's not archival. Even if it says acid free, your printer inks may not be, so these fabrics will eventually suffer from UV damage and fading.

≫ BUBBLE JET SET 2000 AND DIGITAL PRINTING OUT-OF-HOUSE ≪

Now, I am on to you. I know some of you sneaky crafters are thinking, Why not just iron freezer paper onto fabric, run it through a printer, and skip this whole Bubble Jet Set 2000 business? Well, you can, but if the fabric gets wet, it will bleed like crazy. Most inkjet printers do not use inks that are waterproof or colorfast on fabric. You can try a test; in fact, please do. I have heard of crafters who have found the right printer/ink combo and don't use Bubble Jet Set 2000. If your printer accepts colorfast and waterproof pigment-based inks, try to use them. If you give this a whirl, wait for your ink to dry on the fabric, iron it to heat-set it, and then rinse off the excess ink (make sure to place the fabric in a container by itself first).

There are a lot of other ways to transfer images onto fabrics, some using acetone and mediums that I don't describe here. You can learn a lot about this online and in books, but use these materials with caution. They are stinky and in some cases very experimental, so have a sense of adventure. What I am describing here is the best way to achieve clear prints of the original image. If you are into a weathered, distressed look, you might find other methods of image transfer more to your liking. Check the Resources (page 142) for other books on the huge topic of image transfer onto fabric.

Don't want to print it yourself? There are companies that will take your digital image and print it onto fabric for you. The advantage to this is the printing width, often much wider than what you could achieve at home. In some cases it's a normal fabric bolt width—45" (114cm) wide by the number of yards you want. The process is relatively new, and there are still some kinks to work out in terms of color correction. Also, the longevity of these digitally printed fabrics (especially after repeated washings) is still in question. This is worth trying if you are excited by digital printing on fabric, but keep in mind that the resolution for these images is low, so fine lines and details may look fuzzy, and occasionally banding of color can be an issue. Still, it bodes well for exciting things to come in the industry.

APPLYING IRON-ON TRANSFERS

With this method you print or copy your image onto iron-on transfer material, then the image is cut out and ironed directly onto your fabric. In most cases these transfers can be applied to ready-made items like bags, clothes, pillows, and even shoes, if you are daring and have a waterproof medium to paint over them. You can also apply these iron-on transfers to raw fabric and then sew a project with it. Iron-on transfers do require a computer or printer or access to a copy shop. Things to keep in mind before you start: If you're ironing onto a black fabric, you will need opaque transfer sheets, which are very different from normal iron-on sheets and are applied in a different way (see opposite page). Also, the sheets made for inkjet printers, copiers, and laser printers are not interchangeable, so read the descriptions carefully. Some iron-ons are not washable, so pay attention to this, too, especially if you are making these for T-shirts. Finally, most transfers are applied reversed, meaning the mirror image of your artwork. If you don't mind your artwork reversing, this is no big deal, but it will read backward unless you reverse it on your original. A basic word-processing program can reverse text—just search your program's help menu.

A note about ink: Most inkjet printers use dye-based inks, but some newer inkjet printers use pigment-based inks, which can change colors when ironed. Always test first.

MATERIALS

Items or fabric to transfer onto

Iron-on transfer sheets suitable for your printer or copier

Artwork or images ready to transfer

Printer (or access to a copy shop)

TEMPLATE *page 125*

1 Read the manufacturer's instructions for the transfer sheets.

2 Prewash items you will be applying transfers to if they will be laundered.

3 Prepare the image to be transferred, either your own or the template for the design used in this example. Reverse the image if necessary.

4 Load a transfer sheet into the printer and print the image onto it.

5 Iron the transfer sheet onto your fabric (read the manufacturer's instructions).

6 Remove the paper material to expose your image. **A**

WHY THIS METHOD WILL MAKE YOU HAPPY:

★ It's complete instant gratification—and great for kids.

★ It allows you to customize clothes and objects you have on hand with no sewing required.

WHY THIS METHOD MIGHT MAKE YOU SAD:

★ The transfers are a thin plastic material, so they will change the hand, or feel, of the fabric.

★ Even though the transfer material is clear, you will be able to see a faint edge around your image.

★ It's not the cheapest method to use if you need multiples.

APPLYING OPAQUE IRON-ON TRANSFERS

This process is very similar to the normal inkjet transfer material described in the Applying Iron-On Transfers method (see opposite page), but it's for dark fabric and is 100-percent opaque. You don't have to reverse the original image when printing this transfer. I use it for both photos and for applying colored patterns or shapes directly onto my fabric. It's a lot like collage, only with fabric—very fun. This material is for inkjet printers only, not for copiers.

A note about ink: Most inkjet printers use dye-based inks, but some newer inkjet printers are using pigment-based inks, which can change colors when heated. Always test first.

1　Read the manufacturer's instructions for the transfer sheets.

2　Prepare your artwork, either using your own or the template for the design used in this example. If you use the star, you will need to add your photo to its center before you print it out.

3　Prewash items to which you will be applying the transfer if they will be laundered.

4　Test print onto paper. If it looks good, print onto transfer sheet.

5　Cut out your image (read the manufacturer's instructions).

6　Iron onto your fabric using light/medium heat and light pressure at first, despite what the instructions say. You can always turn up the heat. I burned many, many sheets until I learned to turn my iron down.

7　Let it cool and make sure it's well adhered. **A**

WHY THIS METHOD WILL MAKE YOU HAPPY:

★　It's not just for photos! This is a really fun way to make your own patterns and shapes on fabric.

★　Once you test, it's easy to do.

★　You can get great color saturation.

★　It can be used for both fabric yardage and finished items (make sure they can be ironed).

WHY THIS METHOD MIGHT MAKE YOU SAD:

★　It has even more of a plastic-y feel than normal iron-on transfers.

★　It's kind of expensive, especially if you want to make a lot.

★　The transfer may not wear forever on clothes, so launder inside out.

★　These sheets are opaque white, not clear like the normal iron-on sheets. Cut out your image carefully—simple shapes, not text, are best.

MATERIALS

Items or fabric to transfer onto

Opaque inkjet transfer sheets

Artwork or images ready to transfer

Inkjet printer

TEMPLATE *page 126*

SCREEN PRINTING WITH PHOTOEZ

This product for creating silk screens is amazing. You need only the sun and water, and you get the results you would normally expect with photo emulsion, which can be messy, exasperating, time-consuming, and persnickety. Using drawing fluid is great but also very time-consuming and not appropriate for detailed images. A Print Gocco—a small-format silk-screening tool used primarily for making greeting card–sized prints on paper—is an option, but using this to print on fabric can be frustrating, due to the small printing area and the inconsistent results when printing on fabric, not to mention how hard it is to clean and reuse the screens. PhotoEZ allows for a much larger printing area, and the image can be exposed in less than one minute. For real. The screens last indefinitely and are easily cleaned, unlike Print Gocco screens. I used the 8$\frac{1}{2}$" x 11" (21.5 x 28cm) size for projects in the book, but you can get larger sizes and even rolls. Once you try this out, you will be making screens in no time, and you won't believe how easy it is. You might even find yourself forming a band, just to make your shirts!

MATERIALS

Fabric or T-shirts to print onto

PhotoEZ starter kit (the screens, squeegee, and exposure frame); also helpful but not required are the plastic canvas and the plastic frame, all available at EZScreenPrint (see Resources, page 142)

Silk-screen ink for textiles (such as Speedball® Fabric Screen Printing Ink, see Resources, page 142)

9" x 12" (23 x 30.5cm) tub for soaking screen (or a tub larger than screen)

Sulky Spray KK 2000 Temporary Spray Adhesive (optional)

TEMPLATE *page 128*

1   Refer to the manufacturer's instructions for this method. I will list the basic steps and specific advice I have for each step, but use the directions with the kit as your guide.

2   Prepare your artwork. I only use transparencies to burn my screen, not white paper. This results in a quicker screen-burning time and a better black fill. You can get clear transparencies made of your artwork at a copy shop. Make sure the blacks are black and filled as densely as possible.

3   Expose your screen in full sun using the directions with the kit. Afternoon is best; don't try this in the setting sun. The transparencies will expose fully in as little as 50 seconds. If you let them expose for too long, the film won't wash off properly. Test first if you are worried about it.

4   Soak the screen in cool water for at least 30 minutes, touching it as little as possible. Remove from the water and wash off the filler to expose the image areas that were burned. Don't rush this step. Look closely and use a fine brush to really scrub the areas the film burned through, washing both sides. Once you let it dry in the sun again the screen will be set, so make sure all of the excess film is washed away first.

5   Let it dry indoors and then place it in the sun again to set, about 20 minutes or until dry. Now your screen is done! **A**

6 Prewash your shirts, or whatever you are printing onto, and lay out on a table. If you have a plastic frame for your screen (very handy), tape the screen to the back of the frame. This makes it easier to lift.

7 Lightly spray your fabric with Sulky Spray and lay the screen down. Spread the screen printing ink with the squeegee with even pressure over the screen. Lift a corner carefully and look for ink coverage. If there isn't enough, you can carefully lay the screen down and resqueegee. (This is why the spray adhesive is so great.) **B**

8 Remove screen and let the image dry. Heat-set according to manufacturer's directions, and wash. Wash the screen while the paint is still wet to ensure it lasts a long time.

WHY THIS METHOD WILL MAKE YOU HAPPY:

★ For anyone who has tried to print on fabric with a Print Gocco or silk screen using photo emulsion, the benefits of this method will be obvious. There is no easier method with such good results. It's nothing short of life changing.

★ Screen printing is perfect for large quantities; the most time-consuming part is the heat-setting.

★ It's great for crafters wanting custom fabric yardage that's not digitally printed.

★ Once you get the basic kit, all you need to make more is extra screen material. A screen can be burned and ready to use in under an hour—and almost all that time is spent waiting for it to dry.

★ You can print for a fraction of the cost of a Print Gocco.

WHY THIS METHOD MIGHT MAKE YOU SAD:

★ This is not an exact science, but pretty dang close. Expect the print to look a bit handmade. Having said that, it should look very good—if the print is poor, use the troubleshooting guide that comes with the kit.

★ The screen material isn't cheap. It is very inexpensive for how long the screens last (a long, long time) and how much they offer, but if you mess one up, and then another, you will be frustrated. I avoid this by ordering more than I think I will need.

AUNT SARAH AND UNCLE PETE DOLLS

These dolls were originally created with the image of a dear friend of ours who lived far away. My girls were always asking to see Aunt Sarah, and with her living across the country, this was hard. So, the Aunt Sarah dolls were made and are among the most popular toys in the house. Not just for kids, these sweet dolls can go with you on trips or be mailed to loved ones. They are for anyone who needs a reminder of that special someone. Templates are provided for female and male doll bodies; all you need to do is add a photo of a head.

FINISHED SIZE

Uncle Pete: 7³/₄" tall x 1¹/₂" deep x 3" wide at hips (19.5 x 3.8 x 7.5cm)

Aunt Sarah: 7" tall x 1¹/₂" deep x 4" wide at hips (18 x 3.8 x 10cm)

MATERIALS

Front fabric: (1) 8¹/₂" x 11" (20.5 x 28cm) photo fabric sheet for your printer or copier

Backing fabric: (1) 8¹/₂" x 11" (20.5 x 28cm) piece

Photos of heads

Water-soluble or vanishing pen

Poly-fill stuffing

Printer

Sewing machine

TEMPLATE *page 125*

1 Read the Printing Images onto Fabric Sheets method (page 54). Make a color copy of the doll template (or scan and print, or download the PDF from amykarol.com and print) onto regular paper. You will paste your head photo to this sheet of paper.

2 Resize your head photo as necessary by computer or color copier, print it onto paper, and cut it out carefully. Glue the head to the doll template from step 1. **A**

3 If you have a scanner and photo-editing software, scan the photo/doll template, and print it directly onto your photo fabric sheet. If you

AUNT SARAH AND UNCLE PETE DOLLS CONTINUED

don't have a scanner, go to the copy shop and use a color copier to copy it onto your photo fabric sheet. Make 2 copies, just in case.

4 Refer to the manufacturer's instructions regarding heat-setting your image and removing backing paper. Check in which order to do these steps, as it varies by manufacturer.

5 Tape the printed doll sheet onto a window, wrong side facing you, and trace a line on the back around the perimeter of the doll, leaving ½" (13mm) all the way around. This will be your stitching line.

6 Place the doll sheet and the backing fabric right sides together and sew, using a smaller stitch than normal, on your stitching line. Leave the bottom open for stuffing. Trim carefully. Turn right side out and ease out all curves, then stuff with poly-fill. Sew the bottom closed by hand. **B**

TIPS, HINTS, AND OTHER SUGGESTIONS

» These look better if you leave a big margin and loose shape for stuffing and turning. Don't try to sew around the arms exactly.

» These are super cute stuffed in a matching bag or in a basket. They are perfect as going-away gifts for college kids, boyfriends, girlfriends, grandparents—anyone, really.

LUNCH BAG

I love packing a lunch, and I like to do it in style. Why use disposable paper bags when you can reuse supercute ones? Adorn this clever lunch bag with your favorite images from magazines or books. The fabric for this bag has an image scanned from a vintage magazine, complete with a cookie recipe. This project uses only three photo fabric sheets (or homemade sheets with Bubble Jet Set 2000), and the pattern cleverly uses 8½" x 11" (21.5 x 28cm) sheets, so you won't waste any fabric. Once you make one of these, you'll be hooked.

• •

1 Read the Printing Images onto Fabric Sheets method (page 54) or Creating Your Own Fabric Sheets method (page 56). Prepare your artwork by scanning and printing it onto your fabric at home, or make color copies of it and print it onto color copier fabric sheets at the copy shop. You will need 3 printed sheets total.

FINISHED SIZE

10³/₈" high x 6¹/₄" wide x 3¹/₂" deep (26 x 16 x 9cm), unfolded

MATERIALS

Outer bag fabric: (3) 8¹/₂" x 11" (21.5 x 28cm) photo fabric sheets for your printer or copier, or homemade sheets using Bubble Jet Set 2000, cut after printing into:

> *(2) 6¹/₂" x 11" (16.5 x 28cm) front pieces*

> *(2) 4¹/₄" x 11" (11 x 28cm) side pieces*

Lining fabric: ¹/₄ yard (23cm) cut into:

> *(2) 6¹/₂" x 11" (16.5 x 28cm) front pieces*

> *(2) 4¹/₄" x 11" (11 x 28cm) side pieces*

> *(2) 6¹/₂" x 4¹/₂" (16.5 x 11.5cm) bottom ✳*

Binding:

> *(1) 2" x 20" (5 x 51cm) piece of fabric for homemade binding, or, if using premade binding, (1) package (3 yards [2.7m]) of ⁷/₈"- (22mm-) wide single-fold bias tape*

(1) 1" x 2" (2.5 x 5cm) piece of Velcro (optional)

Vintage magazines or other images to copy

Printer

Sewing machine

SEAM ALLOWANCE ¹/₄" (6mm)

✳ One bottom lining piece is used for the bottom of the outer bag.

LUNCH BAG CONTINUED

2 Cut out the outer bag pieces from your printed fabric. Cut out the lining pieces and binding strip if you are making binding. (Skip this step if you are using premade binding.) **A**

3 Make the outer bag: With right sides facing, sew the long sides together on the front and side pieces, creating a box without a top or bottom. With right sides together, pin a lining bottom piece onto the front and side pieces. Sew carefully, flaring out the sides and front, stopping and pivoting with your needle down at each corner.

4 Repeat step 3 with the lining fabric. **B**

5 Turn the outer bag right side out. Place the lining bag inside the outer fabric bag, wrong sides together. This will now look exactly like it will when it is done, minus the binding. Baste around the top edge to keep the layers together.

6 Make binding by ironing your strip in half lengthwise. It will now be 1" x 20" (2.5 x 51cm). Align the raw edges of the binding and the top of the bag and lay out on the printed side of the bag, right sides together. Fold the short end of the tape over so there is no raw edge, and stitch using a $\frac{1}{4}$" (6mm) seam allowance from the edge. Flip the folded edge to the inside on the bag, and hand-stitch it to the lining. **C**

7 To create the closure, machine-stitch one Velcro piece centered just under the binding along the top edge of one front piece. Fold the bag over twice toward the other front piece, and mark where the Velcro touches the other front piece. Stitch the opposite Velcro piece onto the other front piece where the two Velcro pieces would touch.

TIPS, HINTS, AND OTHER SUGGESTIONS

❱❱ You can make this with a vinyl lining. Plastic-coated fabric like oilcloth can be tricky to stitch with, so try a Teflon® presser foot or use masking tape on the edges and sew through all layers to keep the oilcloth from sticking.

❱❱ Create a cute closure by stitching an elastic band into the binding on one side and adding a button on the outside front instead of the Velcro.

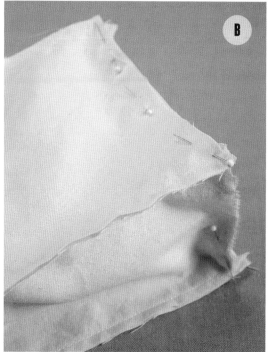

IF MY TOTES COULD SPEAK

Always losing stuff? Me, too. These handy totes can be hung on a wall in your craft room, by your front door, or even inside a closet door—special totes for your special items. This project requires no sewing, just some premade blank totes and iron-on transfer material, making them a super-easy craft for yourself or for gifts.

. . . .

FINISHED SIZE

6" wide x 5³/₄" high (15 x 14.5cm), not including strap

MATERIALS

Small tote bags to print onto (see Resources, page 142)

(2) 8¹/₂" x 11" (21.5 x 28cm) iron-on inkjet transfer sheets

Craft knife or scissors

Printer

TEMPLATE *page 131*

1 Read the Applying Iron-On Transfers method (page 58). Scan or copy the words in the template, or download the PDF at amykarol.com. If you do not have a printer, make color copies of this template onto iron-on transfer sheets meant for color copiers.

2 Print your sheets, trim excess, and iron onto the totes according to the manufacturer's instructions for the iron-on sheets. **A**

TIPS, HINTS, AND OTHER SUGGESTIONS

》 Make your own words or phrases by using a basic word-processing program. Make sure to reverse the text (and check in a mirror) before you iron onto your fabric.

》 Try making individualized totes, using the names of your family members or your roommates.

》 Don't limit yourself to words. Photos and artwork can be applied in this way; just remember to reverse your original images or they will be a mirror image of what you are used to seeing, which may not be a big deal.

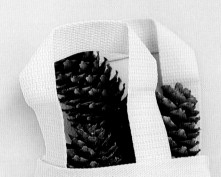

loose change

none of your business

keys

might be garbage

BABY PILLOW

A custom pillow for baby makes a wonderful gift for a stylin' nursery. This linen pillow cover is embellished with opaque iron-on images in a cool, modern way. Below are the directions for sewing the pillow cover, but you can use a purchased pillow with a cotton or linen cover and make this a no-sew project. Either way, it's easy and very quick—but will be cherished forever.

FINISHED SIZE
Approximately 13" wide x 13" high x 4" deep (33 x 33 x 10cm)

MATERIALS
½ yard (46cm) pillow cover fabric (if not using a pillow that came with a cover) cut into:

> *(1) 14" x 14" (35.5 x 35.5cm) piece for front*

> *(2) 14" x 12" (35.5 x 30.5cm) pieces for back*

Opaque iron-on inkjet sheets

14" x 14" (35.5 x 35.5cm) pillow insert

Sewing machine

Printer

SEAM ALLOWANCE *¼" (6mm)*

TEMPLATE *page 135*

1   Read the Applying Opaque Iron-On Transfers method (page 59). Make the pillow cover by cutting out the pattern pieces from the fabric. Hem one of the 14" (35.5cm) edges on each 14" x 12" (35.5 x 30.5cm) back piece by turning $\frac{1}{2}$" (13mm) over twice and topstitching. Repeat with the other back piece. **A**

2   Lay out pieces as follows: first the pillow front, right side facing up. Next, a back piece with the hemmed edge toward the middle of the pillow and the raw edge aligned with the bottom of the front, wrong side up. Lastly, the remaining back piece, with the hemmed edge toward the middle of the pillow and the raw edge aligning with the top edge of the front pillow, wrong side up. (These hemmed pieces will make the opening for the pillow to slip into—what you are making here is a pillow envelope.) Pin and stitch around all 4 edges. Trim if needed and turn right side out. **B**

3   Copy the colored patterns from the template either by scanning and printing onto the opaque transfer paper or by printing the PDF of the template at amykarol.com. If you want to include your baby's name, add the text at this time, by creating the text on your computer and printing it directly onto the sheets.

4   Cut out your desired shapes: Use the templates provided or make up your own by using the colored patterns any old way. Iron onto your pillow. Let cool and slip in your pillow insert. **C**

TIPS, HINTS, AND OTHER SUGGESTIONS

≫   This material is great for dark fabrics, so use it to its advantage and try it on black.

≫   This material might lift over time. If this happens, carefully iron again, using a pressing cloth.

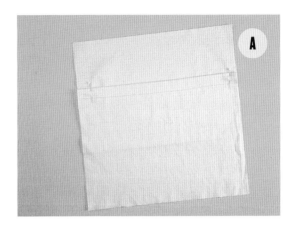

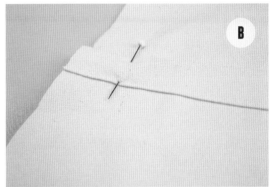

WATERCOLOR TOTE

Does the idea of painting directly onto fabric kind of freak you out? Then this is the perfect project for you. Don't worry about this watercolor look being hard; it's not. You make a painting first and then print it onto your fabric. You have total control and end up with a one-of-a-kind tote that you can actually recreate again and again, if you want to. This bag is designed to use 8½" x 11" (21.5 x 28cm) fabric sheets from your printer or copier, making it even easier. The tote is two pieces and the strap is one long piece that when stitched on creates the bottom and the sides. An asymmetrical knot gives this whole project an arty-cool touch.

FINISHED SIZE
10" high x 7" wide x 3" deep (25.5 x 18 x 7.5cm), not including strap. Strap extends about 36" (91cm) on left side and 9" (23cm) on right, untied.

MATERIALS
(2) photo fabric sheets for a printer or copier (or homemade sheets using Bubble Jet Set 2000)

¼ yard (23cm) bag lining and inner strap fabric cut into:

> *(1) 86" x 4" length (218.5 x 10cm) piece for inner strap (or sew shorter pieces together to get this length)*

> *(2) 8½" x 11" (21.5 x 28cm) pieces for lining* ✱

¼ yard (23cm) outer strap fabric cut into: (1) 86" x 4" length (218.5 x 10cm) piece

Printer

Sewing machine

SEAM ALLOWANCE *¼" (6mm)*

PATTERN *page 137*

TEMPLATE *page 138*

✱ This bag's construction is probably like nothing you have done before. You line the front and back of the bag separately. Then you make the super-long strap and then, as the last step, you sew the strap to the bag front and back (which are already lined). The strap forms the bottom and the sides of the bag.

1. Read the Printing Images onto Fabric Sheets method (page 54). Prepare original artwork by making a simple watercolor painting on 8$\frac{1}{2}$" x 11" (20.5 x 28cm) paper (or make a copy of the template). Scan this original and print at home on fabric sheets, or take to a copy shop and use fabric sheets designed for a color copier. Make 2 copies, one for each side of the bag. **A**

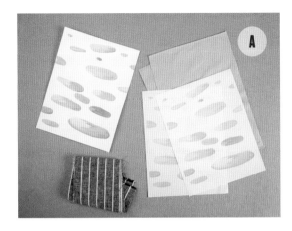

2. Cut out the pieces for the bag lining and inner and outer straps. Make front and back of bag by placing the right sides of the printed fabric and the lining fabric together and sewing all the way around, leaving a small opening in the top for turning right side out. Repeat with the second printed fabric sheet and lining piece. Trim and turn right side out. Topstitch across the top edge of front and back pieces, closing the opening as you stitch across. Do this on the top only; the sides will be stitched to the strap.

3. Make the strap by piecing the strips together to make the full 86" (218.5cm) length, if necessary. Sew the outer and inner strap fabric together, right sides facing; taper in the ends as shown on the pattern. Leave a small opening on one side to turn right side out. Turn and iron flat. **B**

4. Complete the bag by pinning the bag front 37" (94cm) from one strap tip. Starting on one edge with the right sides facing, stitch all the way around the 3 sides on the printed fabric, pivoting at corners. Continue stitching down the strap to the tip. Repeat on back side of bag, attaching the back the same way. Stitch remaining strap, closing as you stitch across. **C**

5. Turn the bag right side out and tie the strap into a knot, which will be asymmetrically placed. **D**

TIPS, HINTS, AND OTHER SUGGESTIONS

≫ You can use any design, not just watercolor. Try painting, collage, or even just copying a newspaper or magazine.

≫ Changing the length of these straps will change the bag; you can make a shorter-strapped tote the same way.

BAND T-SHIRTS!

In keeping with the time-honored tradition of making band T-shirts before your band has played live or possibly even rehearsed, I bring you this easy project. No long exposure times, tedious drawing fluid, or crummy screens to fight with—these T-shirts can be made in a snap once you have copied your artwork onto a transparency. Using a silk-screen method that requires much less time and labor than traditional methods, you will have your own band merch in no time. You can design your own from scratch, use this design and add your band name, or use this design as is. Start practicing!

1 Read the Screen Printing with PhotoEZ method (page 60). Prepare artwork (either yours or the template) by copying it onto a transparency at a copy shop. **A**

2 Expose the screen according to the manufacturer's instructions.

3 Soak, rinse, and dry the screen according to the manufacturer's instructions. **B**

4 Prewash and dry your T-shirts. Stabilize the image area with freezer paper on the inside of the T-shirt (page 37). Lightly spray each T-shirt with spray adhesive. Position the screen and apply the ink to the shirt with the kit's squeegee. Lift carefully to check for coverage, applying more ink if necessary.

5 Let dry and heat-set using the silk-screen ink manufacturer's instructions.

TIPS, HINTS, AND OTHER SUGGESTIONS

》 Resist the urge to use normal textile paint with the screen. It will dry too quickly and cause many headaches.

》 For events and gifts, it's nice to print onto shirts that people will be comfortable in. To keep sizing guesswork at a minimum, ask people to provide their own shirts so you know they will fit.

MATERIALS

Fabric or T-shirts to print onto

PhotoEZ starter kit (the screens, squeegee, and exposure frame); also helpful but not required are the plastic canvas and the plastic frame, all available at EZScreenPrint (see Resources, page 142)

Silk-screen ink for textiles (such as Speedball Fabric Screen Printing Ink, see Resources, page 142)

9" x 12" (23 x 30.5cm) tub for soaking screen

Freezer paper

Sulky Spray KK 2000 Temporary Spray Adhesive (optional, but very helpful)

TEMPLATE *page 132*

MODERN BEDSHEETS

Ever since I fell in love with paper cutting, or *scherenschnitte*, I have been working on a way to reproduce these designs on fabric. PhotoEZ makes this painless. I have provided the artwork for this no-sew project, so all you need are some bedsheets and pillowcases, either new or ones your already have, and the PhotoEZ materials. No paper cutting is even needed! Once you see how easy this is to reproduce, you will want to try it with your own designs. Have fun!

. . . .

MATERIALS

PhotoEZ starter kit (the screens, squeegee, and exposure frame); also helpful but not required are the plastic canvas and the plastic frame, all available at EZScreenPrint (see Resources, page 142)

Silk-screen ink for textiles (such as Speedball Fabric Screen Printing Ink, see Resources, page 142)

Bedsheets to fit your bed; a top sheet and 2 pillowcases are shown

9" x 12" (23 x 30.5cm) tub for soaking screen

Sulky Spray KK 2000 Temporary Spray Adhesive (optional, but very helpful)

TEMPLATE *page 139*

1 Read the Screen Printing with PhotoEZ method (page 60). Prepare artwork by copying it onto a transparency at a copy shop. Prewash and dry your bedsheets.

2 Expose the screen according to the manufacturer's instructions.

3 Soak, rinse, and dry the screen according to the manufacturer's instructions.

4 Working on the pillowcase hems first, lightly spray with spray adhesive. Position the screen and apply the ink with the kit's squeegee. Lift carefully to check for coverage, applying more ink if necessary. Repeat image across the pillow, blow-drying as you go to speed the drying process. Repeat on the top sheet hem. **A**

5 Let dry and heat-set according to the silk-screen ink directions. **B**

TIPS, HINTS, AND OTHER SUGGESTIONS

>> With this project you print several times to create the pattern. You can speed the drying with a blow-dryer. You can try to lay a clean sheet of paper over the first print as you work on the next one, but this might smudge, so it's best to blow-dry. It's okay if the repeats don't line up perfectly; it's part of the charm. When you get to the edge of the bedsheet, slide a sheet of paper to screen onto, so the ink can be applied to the very edge of the bedsheet. The extra ink will print on the paper.

>> Avoid printing on the part of a pillow where a head might actually go. The inks shouldn't smell bad, especially after they are washed, but I wouldn't want to rub my face on them.

5

DYE IT
NO. I DON'T MEAN TIE-DYE.
I PROMISE.

★ ★

Forget what you know about dyeing. We all remember bleaching jeans at home or tie-dyeing T-shirts at summer camp. That was then. Now we have professional-grade dyes that are colorfast, bright, beautiful, and easily applied. You can use your washing machine or just a plastic bucket. Many fiber-art books include long lists of chemical supplies and detailed directions, but really, it's not that hard. You need very few supplies to get the look you want, most of which you already have. Even more exciting, you can now buy textile paints that act like dye! They are applied just like paint, making it even easier. Once you get comfortable with dyes, you will think twice about everything in your closet. Hand-me-downs and thrift finds gain new appeal, and you'll have a ton of fun while you transform them. Just don't forget: Dye will stain. That's what it is for, after all—so wear an apron or some grubbies. Before you start, please read the Dye Safety section, okay? It's on page 82.

BASIC SMALL-QUANTITY DYEING

There are many ways to dye fabric, but the most basic is tub dyeing. If the quantities are really small, you can even dye in a bowl or a cup. I have dyed in many other ways, and I keep coming back to this basic method for small-quantity dyeing. I learned it while dyeing fat quarters of fabric for my quilts, and I discovered it works well for all sorts of projects. One note: For clothing, it's best to dye in the washing machine if you want even color coverage. If you don't mind the mottled look, then don't worry about it and go for tub dyeing. If the supply list and directions here freak you out, please don't skip dyeing! Try using iDye in your washing machine instead (see page 84).

When I say *small quantities,* I mean one T-shirt or some ribbon, lace, or other trims. Or a few baby onesies and socks—that type of thing. Imagine what could slosh around freely in a bucket you have on hand. That's the amount I am talking about. If your item is bigger, use a bigger bucket. You get the idea.

MATERIALS
Fabric materials to dye

Fabric dye—Procion MX or iDye (see iDye sidebar on page 84)

Soda ash

Synthrapol (optional but recommended)

Old plastic bags (one for each color)

Dust mask

Rubber gloves

Plastic drop cloth (optional)

Plastic measuring spoons (used only for dye, not for food, ever)

3–5 gallon (12–15l) plastic tub or bucket for presoaking items

5½ quart (5.2l) plastic shoe bin–sized tub or bucket. For fat quarters of fabric (22" x 18" pieces [56 x 47.5cm]), a 12 oz (340g) plastic drinking cup is perfect.

1 Prewash all items to be dyed, either by hand (for lace or ribbon) or in the washing machine, with 1 teaspoon soda (5ml) ash and 1 teaspoon (5ml) Synthrapol per 3 yards (2.7m) of fabric. Don't dry. Next, put on your gloves and soak the items in a 3–5 gallon (12–15l) plastic tub in a mix of 1 gallon (3.8l) hot water and 1 cup (8oz) dissolved soda ash. Let the items soak at least 30 minutes, longer if you want to. You can keep this solution for a few months, so store the extra solution in a container, and label accordingly.

2 Put on a dust mask, and add anywhere from 1 to 3 teaspoons (5ml–15ml) of dye to a little warm water in a small cup. Stir to make a paste. When fully dissolved, add 1 cup (237ml) of water. The darker the color you want to achieve, the more dye you will need.

3 Test with a scrap of fabric if you have one. Now, add your fabric item to the mixture and swirl it around several times, squeezing and refolding, making sure the item is saturated with dye. When fully saturated, lift it out of the dye bath (don't squeeze out the dye) and

put it in a plastic bag to cure, or leave it in the cup if only dyeing a bit of fabric. For best results, let the dye set for 3 hours or more. To make a set of graduated colors, add water to the original dye bath, using more water with each fabric, creating a lighter color each time.

4   Take the fabric out of the bag or cup and rinse in a clean tub with several changes of water until the water runs clear. Wash items in the washing machine using Synthrapol—$\frac{1}{2}$ teaspoon (2.5ml) per yard (0.9m) of fabric; very little is needed. Line-dry or place in the dryer on normal heat. **A**

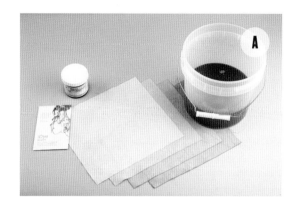

WHY THIS METHOD WILL MAKE YOU HAPPY:

★   Dyeing is magic. Nothing is more thrilling than giving fabric a new color. You will become addicted to this, and nothing will be safe.

★   Learning this quick method is easy and takes very little time. Stock up on white and dyeable items so you have them handy when you want to get that color you can't find in existing trims.

WHY THIS METHOD MIGHT MAKE YOU SAD:

★   The unpredictable nature of dyeing can be a perfectionist's worst nightmare. Take diligent notes so you can recreate a color you fall in love with—or just loosen up. Use the note-taking template on page 130.

★   It only takes a second to dye something the wrong color. Oops. If you are nervous about the dye being too dark, make it easy on yourself and make your dye bath lighter than you think you want. You can always add more dye. Always test with a scrap piece of fabric first, and remember, it will look lighter when it dries.

★   Wash your freshly dyed items separately from clothes for a while until you are sure all of the dye is removed.

TIPS, HINTS, AND OTHER SUGGESTIONS

»   Don't try to cover up a badly stained item with dye—it won't work. It will just create a different-colored item. Trust me.

»   Try over-dyeing fabrics. This means taking patterned fabrics and dyeing

BASIC SMALL-QUANTITY DYEING CONTINUED

them. It's a great way to change your stash, especially if you dye a bunch of fabrics together in the same dye bath. Somehow they will all work together. It's magic!

» Hey, parents and friends of small people! Have you seen colored silk play scarves for kids and babies? Dye them yourself using this method and blank, ready-to-dye silk scarves (see Resources, page 142). They are wonderful toys, make great gifts, and are a fraction of the price if you dye them yourself. Really wash that excess dye out, though—babies chew on these and you don't want dye in there!

» DYE SAFETY, OR A BIT ABOUT MATERIALS THAT MIGHT CREEP YOU OUT «

Safe-to-use dyes are available, but you still need to use caution. First, read about the dyes you are using—some say nontoxic, some don't. Almost all dye brands have websites now with lots of information (and some really good dyeing directions, too), so it's worth doing some research.

Always wear a mask when handling dye powder, even if it's a nontoxic dye. Gloves are important as well, so put them on. This isn't just so your fingers stay clean; gloves are a barrier to prevent dye from seeping into your skin. When making the projects in this chapter, try working outside or where there is good ventilation. Use tubs, buckets, spoons, and measuring cups dedicated to dyeing only, and label accordingly. Don't use these items in the kitchen once they have been used for dyeing.

There are many books and resources out there on making natural dyes, which is wonderful. If you go down this road for health reasons, make sure you are using a safe mordant (the ingredient that allows the dye stick to the fabric). Some mordants used in natural dyeing are toxic, contrary to what you might think.

I don't mix dyes of any kind when I am nursing or pregnant. This might be an unnecessary precaution, especially because I use nontoxic dyes, but I would rather be safe. I ask a friend to mix the dye when it's powdered, and then I step in only to check the dye bath—I don't handle the dye or dye fabric at all.

The only supply that I would caution you on safety-wise is the bleach pen. It's a cool effect, but it *is* bleach. Creepy bleach with creepy ingredients. The fumes are largely contained in the pen, but use this tool outside if you can, and keep kids and pets away while you are working.

PAINTING WITH DYE

Some products bridge the worlds of paint and dye. These are paints that act like dyes, and in many cases are the best of both. They have the consistency of water and can be applied wet-on-wet to achieve watercolor-like effects on fabric. I have included this method in the dye section, even though it is actually an acrylic paint product, because it behaves so much like a dye. Here's why this stuff is so cool: Paint typically changes the hand of the fabric because it lays on the surface. A dye penetrates the fiber, so there is no change in the texture, which is the best-case scenario. But to use dye as paint is a bit tricky. You may have to thicken dyes with chemicals or starches, test like crazy, and then apply an afterwash to keep the color from bleeding. There's a lot to do, and it can be a drag. Or you can use this acrylic paint product. Use it straight from the bottle, or mix it with water. You can even mix it with other textile paints; it will just thicken a bit more. You can use it on silk, cotton, and linen. You'll need to heat-set it (see the directions on the bottle) and then follow with a little Synthrapol in a wash. It barely changes the hand of the fabric. This products works best wet-on-wet, so keep a mister or spray bottle handy, and go with the flow.

1 Prewash and dry your fabric to remove all sizings, which are finishes that are often applied to fabric. This step is especially important because any finish left on fabric can interfere with the dye. If you want a very loose watercolor look, you can paint on the fabric after you wash it but before you dry it. Make sure to run it through the spin cycle or squeeze out as much water as possible.

2 Prep your work area by laying a towel on a tabletop, or use a padded work surface. Stretch the fabric over the table, securing with pins or weights and smoothing out wrinkles.

3 Using a plastic bottle with a spray attachment, spray your fabric to moisten it if it's not already damp from the prewash. Let the water soak in while you mix your paint.

4 Pour the paint onto a large palette or into several small cups. Mix your desired colors. Mix more than you think you will need, because the fabric soaks up a lot of paint.

5 Apply paint to the fabric with a brush, squeeze bottle, sprayer, or sponges—your choice. You can layer applications, but for a soft look, work on the fabric only while it's wet. **A**

6 Let air dry, and heat-set with an iron (according to the paint manufacturer's instructions).

MATERIALS

Fabric to dye

Dye-Na-Flow or Setacolor Transparent Colors textile paint (dilute Setacolor with water to thin) in assorted colors (it's mixable, so you only need red, blue, yellow, white, and black if you are comfortable mixing your own colors. See page 15 for info on this.)

Plastic bottle with spray or mister attachment

Small cups or a palette

Synthrapol (optional)

Brushes of various sizes, or other application tools—squeeze bottle, sprayer, or sponges

PAINTING WITH DYE CONTINUED

7 Wash with Synthrapol or another nonbleach detergent in cool water to remove any extra paint.

WHY THIS METHOD WILL MAKE YOU HAPPY:

★ What's not to love about a watercolor effect on fabric? This forgiving method is much easier to work with than traditional dyes mixed with thickening agents.

WHY THIS METHOD MIGHT MAKE YOU SAD:

★ This is truly a one-of-a-kind technique, so no mass-production options here. If you want to recreate a watercolor look multiple times, try using the Printing Images onto Fabric Sheets method used for the Watercolor Tote, page 72.

TIPS, HINTS, AND OTHER SUGGESTIONS

» Use the tightest fabric weave possible for the smoothest look. Think bedsheets.

» This takes a while. Use this method as an accent on fabric instead of trying to paint the whole piece.

» Practice and test on scraps first! Really, you will be happy you did. And don't be surprised if you like your scraps a whole lot. Keep them.

» iDYE «

So, you are interested in dyeing, but not so interested in all the fuss. Remember the good old days when you could just throw your jeans and T-shirts in the wash with a box of dye from the grocery store, and voilà, you were done? The dyes back then weren't that vibrant, but the effort was minimal. Well, you can still do this with much better results. Jacquard has a one-time-use dye packet called iDye, and all you need is some salt, maybe some vinegar, and a washing machine. That's it. The packet will dye about 3 lbs (1.4kg) of fabric, and you don't need gloves, chemicals, or even special soap. All you need to know is how to stop the water from filling up too much in your washing machine and how to extend the time on it. The colors are great, and there is a huge range of them. This dye will work on blended fabric, too, but the directions are a little different if you aren't using 100-percent natural fibers, so read the packet first. These colors are not as vibrant as Procion MX dyes, and they may fade a bit more over time, but they are a vast improvement over what has been available for quick no-measure, no-fuss dyeing in the past. See the Resources on page 142 to get some for yourself, and start dyeing.

PAINTING WITH DYE USING A RESIST

Now that you are loving paints that act like dyes, get the most out of them by using them with a resist. A resist does just that: It resists being dyed. When you draw with the resist, it acts as a barrier, allowing you to paint shapes and lines with crisp edges. Wherever the resist is applied, the fabric will show through. There are all kinds of resists out there. Some of them are toxic, some are not; some wash out, and some you have to steam away. To make your life easier, use a water-based resist. These are safe and wash out with a good scrub of soapy water. This gel-like liquid is best applied with a squeeze bottle, but don't feel tied to that; once you try it, you will come up with different application techniques.

1   Transfer any designs using a water-soluble pen or vanishing pen onto the fabric.

2   Pour water-based resist into a small squeeze bottle with a metal tip or a fine squeeze tip. (Sometimes I find the metal tips too small and prefer a standard squeeze bottle tip.)

3   Draw over the marked lines with the resist, making sure the resist soaks the cloth completely. The line will spread as it dries, quite a bit if you squeeze out a lot, so keep this in mind and do lots of testing.

4   Look closely at the lines before painting. Anywhere the resist breaks, paint will leak through. Fill in with more resist as necessary.

5   After the resist has dried (you can speed this up with a hair dryer), mix your fabric paint. Your lines might be hard to see when dry, but they will show up again when you dampen the fabric. Mist the fabric with water and let saturate for about 5 minutes. Apply the paint onto the damp fabric and watch it flow—you will notice how it stops at the resist's edges. **A**

6   Let the paint dry, and heat set using an iron. When dry, remove the resist with soapy water and a little elbow grease; it takes a bit of scrubbing to get it off. **B**

MATERIALS

Prewashed fabric

Dye-Na-Flow or Setacolor Transparent Colors textile paint

Jacquard Clear Water Based Resist or Inkodye Resist

Small squeeze bottle with metal tip (5–9mm)

Water-soluble or vanishing pen

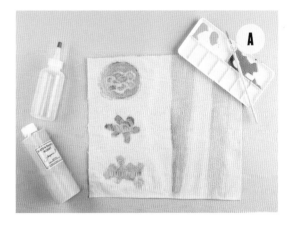

WHY THIS METHOD WILL MAKE YOU HAPPY:

★   This is watercolor with a safety net. Think coloring book—draw the lines and fill it in. Super easy and super simple.

★   You can add dye to the resist so your lines will be colored, not clear. So many options!

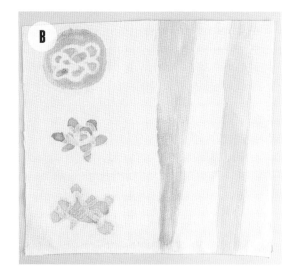

PAINTING WITH DYE USING A RESIST CONTINUED

★ This is a nice way to add a handmade look to existing light-colored clothes.

★ Both Dye-Na-Flow Silk Paint and Setacolor Transparent Colors are nontoxic. In the past, gutta and other resists have been made with icky ingredients. It's wonderful that nontoxic options are now available.

★ No steaming is necessary to set the color, which was formerly often the case. Another wonderful bonus!

WHY THIS METHOD MIGHT MAKE YOU SAD:

★ If you are a tinkerer and like to fuss with things, you can get frustrated with this technique. You need to paint with a light hand and stop. Put the brush down. I mean it. The more you go back and paint over, the muddier and less delicate your color will be.

★ It's hard to know when to stop with this, and painting takes a long time, so try this on small projects before you try it on something huge.

TIPS, HINTS, AND OTHER SUGGESTIONS

» This works beautifully on silk. You can buy ready-to-paint silk scarves (see Resources, page 142) and use this technique, skipping all of the traditional silk painting and steaming.

REMOVING DYE WITH A BLEACH PEN

You can achieve really wonderful effects with a bleach pen on fabric. Traditionally with discharge work on fabric (*discharge* is removing dye from fabric to make a design), you need to mix icky chemicals or thicken bleach to make pastes or a bleach stop. The whole process is messy and involves fumes—a lot of work for a fifteen-minute project. Using a bleach pen takes all of the pain out of this cool technique. Just use it like a pen on dark fabric, wait, and wash it out.

1 Transfer any design you want to outline to your fabric, or draw directly onto your fabric.

2 Shake the bleach pen and push a metal tip onto the end. (It won't fit

all the way on, which is okay; just make sure it doesn't leak.) Hold the bleach pen like a pencil, and test a line on a scrap piece of cloth. Let it rest for 30 minutes and rinse with water. Check it out—does it look okay? Now you can work on the real piece of fabric. **A**

3 On the real fabric, follow the transferred or drawn line with the bleach pen and let it dry in a well-ventilated room (or better yet, outside) for about 30 minutes. Rinse with soapy water and let dry. If working on existing clothes, run through a wash cycle and hang dry or pop into the dryer on medium heat.

WHY THIS METHOD WILL MAKE YOU HAPPY:

★ This effect is so easy, you will find yourself looking at solid fabrics in a different way. The bleaching isn't always white, so the unexpected color that comes though adds to the fun.

★ You don't always have to use blacks/browns/blues. Oranges and reds work well, too. Try a yellow! Just make sure the fabric is an intense color.

WHY THIS METHOD MIGHT MAKE YOU SAD:

★ This is straight-up bleach, kids, so it's toxic. Not good for anyone sensitive to fumes. Work in a well-ventilated area and let it dry outside if you can.

★ The lines you draw with a bleach pen do grow and thicken as they rest, so have loose expectations of your design and be willing to experiment. It's not good for precise lines that need to be detailed. Try a finer metal tip and squeeze the pen less if your lines get too thick. Sometimes the line will look like it's barely there at first, but after 30 minutes it appears as a perfect thin line, so test first.

TIPS, HINTS, AND OTHER SUGGESTIONS

» Bleach can ruin rayon and silk fibers, so use this bleach pen only on sturdy cottons and denims.

MATERIALS
Dark cotton fabric

Clorox® Bleach Pen®

Metal tips (#5–#9 according to preference)

Light-colored transfer pencil or transfer tracing paper for dark fabrics

TEMPLATES *page 123*

THE PROJECTS

DON'T TOSS IT, DYE IT!

You know which clothing item I am talking about. That one. The one you bought that was never quite right. It fit, but never really felt like you. Now you are cleaning and need to get rid of some clothes, and there it sits, neglected. Don't toss it! This is the perfect way to jump into dyeing. If you don't like the color it turns out, fine, toss it in your donation pile, give it to a friend, cut it up and make it into something else—but try to dye it first. You have nothing to lose.

MATERIALS

An old blouse or another clothing item from your closet

Procion MX dye or iDye

Soda ash (if using Procion dye)

Synthrapol (if using Procion dye)

Gloves/aprons (if using Procion dye)

3–5 gallon (12–15l) plastic tub to dye in

New or vintage buttons (make sure they fit in the buttonholes before you sew them on)

1 Read the Basic Small-Quantity Dyeing method (page 80). Grab your not-quite-right clothing item and make sure it's clean. If it's not, wash it but don't dry it. **A**

2 Mix up the dye bath using the directions in the Basic Small-Quantity Dyeing method using either Procion dye or the very simple iDye. After presoaking if your dyeing method requires it, add your garment to the dye bath.

3 Once dyed, wash the garment several times and then dry. Now add fancy new buttons if you like. **B**

TIPS, HINTS, AND OTHER SUGGESTIONS

》 Lace trims, ribbons, and appliquéd flowers are another way to make a clothing item special. If your dye didn't cover evenly, you can use these elements to camouflage imperfect areas as well. (Shhhh.)

PREPPY KERCHIEF

This sweet kerchief is perfect for covering up your bad hair days. A triangle of linen is painted with dye and finished with a premade cream binding that also creates the ties. By folding and painting the fabric, you get a lovely sophisticated look with minimal effort. Make two at once by painting a square of fabric, then cutting it diagonally to make two kerchiefs. How easy is that? It's perfect for gifts and is a great way to use up your fabric stash.

• •

1 Read the Painting with Dye method (page 83). Cut a square of kerchief fabric 15" x 15" (38 x 38cm). Mist fabric with water until it's lightly damp.

2 Fold the fabric in an accordion style in 1" (2.5cm) increments and secure with binder clips. Don't worry if it's not perfectly even.

3 Using the green dye straight from the bottle, paint along the tops of the folds. Let dry. (Use a hair dryer if you are impatient.) When it's dry, unclip and iron to heat-set. **A**

4 For the second color in the opposite direction, accordion fold in the opposite direction. Mix a little yellow with the green and paint the folds the same way described above, securing with the binder clips. Let dry, unclip, and heat-set with an iron.

5 Cut the kerchief square diagonally in half. Hem the 2 short sides of each by turning over ¼" (6mm) twice, ironing flat, and topstitching. Trim off any extra overhang at each corner created by turning the hem up. Leave the long side unhemmed.

6 Cut a 46" (117cm) length of bias tape. Center the unhemmed edge of the kerchief on the unfolded tape. Fold the bias tape in half over the edge of the kerchief. It will now be ¼" (6mm) wide on each side. You should have approximately 15" (38cm) of loose bias tape extending beyond the corners of the kerchief to make the ties. **B**

FINISHED SIZE
20½" wide x 10" deep (52 x 25.5cm); bias tape extends about 12" (30.5cm) on each side

MATERIALS
½ yard (46cm) light-colored linen or cotton fabric (not too heavy—think pillowcase weight—an old pillowcase would work perfectly and would make 4 kerchiefs)

Dye-Na-Flow textile paint in green and yellow (or the colors of your choice)

1 package ½"- (13mm-) wide single-fold bias tape (a 4-yard (3.7m) package will trim 2 kerchiefs)

4–6 binder clips (the kind from an office supply shop)

Spray bottle of water for misting fabric

Sewing machine

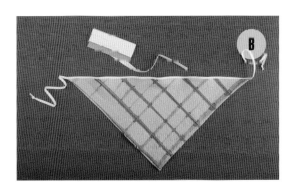

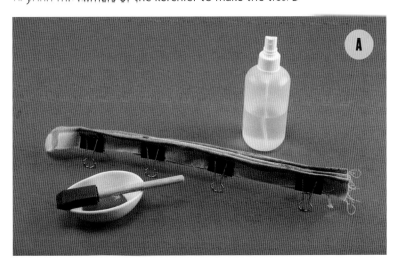

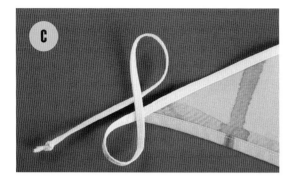

PREPPY KERCHIEF CONTINUED

7 Pin the tape to the fabric to secure. Starting at one end of the kerchief, stitch on the tape using a zigzag stitch approximately the width of the tape, so you catch all layers while stitching. After you reach the end of the kerchief, continue sewing over the end of the tape to make the ties. Repeat with the length of tie at the opposite end of the kerchief. Tie a knot on each end of the ties to secure. **C**

TIPS, HINTS, AND OTHER SUGGESTIONS

» Trim one of the triangles down for a matching kid's size. Try a 13" x 13" (33 x 33cm) square for a youth size.

» When sewing the bias tape onto the kerchief, don't pull the fabric. This edge is cut on the bias and can stretch easily.

» This is a great dyed look for all types of sewing projects and would look smashing on a dress. If you are working with large pieces of fabric, try securing the folded fabric with woodworking tension clamps.

SOFT ART: WHOLE-CLOTH QUILT

This is a project for you to get all arty with. It's pretty much just painting on a big piece of fabric—one big piece. Then you make a sandwich with batting and a backing fabric and sew it all together—no binding to worry about. Quilt it by tying it off with yarn, and that's it. This is endlessly customizable; the size and design can be changed to your heart's content. The only real techniques to learn are tying-off (super easy) and getting comfortable enough to actually paint on a huge piece of fabric. You might want to try this outside on a sunny day, ideally on a big table, or get all crazy and work on the floor—that's what Jackson Pollock did.

FINISHED SIZE
Approximately 50" x 41" (127 x 104cm)—a perfect lap-size quilt.

MATERIALS
1¹/₂ yards (137cm) light-colored quilting cotton fabric for top

1¹/₂ yards (137cm) backing fabric; quilting cotton or flannel works well

1¹/₂ yards (137cm) batting of your choice

Dye-Na-Flow textile paint in red, yellow, and white (or the colors of your choice)

1 skein Lion Brand Wool Ease Yarn, 80% acrylic, 20% wool, 3 oz (85g); 197 yards (180m), in Burgundy (4), or similar yarn of your choice

Large needle (darning or curved)

Water-based resist (see Resources, page 142)

Plastic bottle with a narrow tip (not metal)

Water-soluble or vanishing pen

Plastic bottle with mister attachment

Straightledge

Sewing machine

TEMPLATE *page 139*

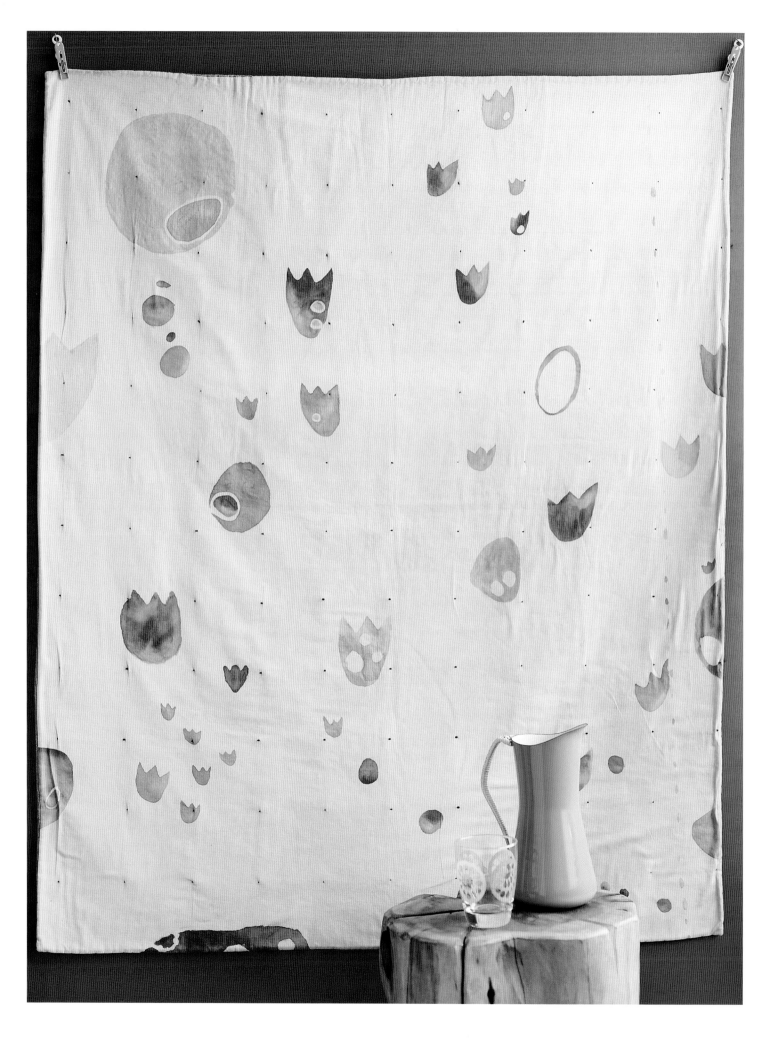

SOFT ART: WHOLE-CLOTH QUILT CONTINUED

1 Read the Painting with Dye Using a Resist method (page 85). Prewash all fabrics. Transfer template designs onto the fabric top with a water-soluble pen, using the overall photo as a guide for placement. (Or do your own thing!) Trace shapes with the resist. Let the resist dry. When dry, mist water inside the shapes; it's okay if it's just in the general area. Paint with dye while the fabric is wet. Let dry and heat-set using an iron. **A**

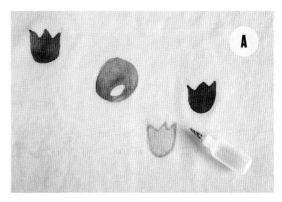

2 Lay out the quilt pieces as follows: backing fabric, right side facing up; then the painted quilt top, right side facing down; then the batting on top. Secure with pins and stitch through all thicknesses with a $^3/_8$" (9mm) seam allowance around the edges, leaving a generous opening for turning right side out. Trim excess seam allowance and turn right side out. Hand-stitch the opening closed and iron flat.

3 With a straightedge and water-soluble pen, make a mark every 4" (10cm) in rows 4" (10cm) apart. Using yarn and a needle (time to put on that thimble!), sew big basting stitches between the marks, stitching $^1/_4$" (6mm) at each mark, through all layers. When you have completed each row, snip the yarn lengths in the middle of the loop and tie in a double knot at each spot. Trim knot tails to $^3/_4$" (2cm) long. **B** On the top of the quilt, you will see tiny $^1/_4$" (6mm) stitches. **C**

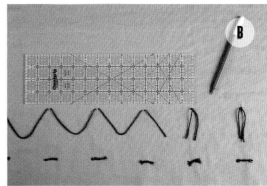

4 Wash and dry the quilt to give it a worn-in look and feel.

TIPS, HINTS, AND OTHER SUGGESTIONS

» You can tie your knots on either the top or bottom; quilters do it either way.

» Tying off a quilt is great for crafters who don't want to dive into machine- or hand-quilting, but it's not as fast as you think. Put on a movie and prepare to be at it for a while.

» This technique is wonderful for whole pieces of fabric you don't want to detract from visually. You can skip the painting part of this project and use a fun novelty print.

» Cotton or wool yarn will eventually fray and felt, whereas acrylic and acrylic-blended yarn won't. I don't mind the felting, but many quilters use acrylic yarn to avoid this.

STRIPED SKIRT

This is discharge dyeing the easy way. Instead of mixing up messy bleach and painting with a brush, just grab a handy bleach pen fitted with a metal tip and you are ready to go. No pattern is needed for this sweet 1950s-style full gathered skirt. Just take your waist measurement and multiply it by 3. This will make a very full skirt with a ton of flounce. If you are using a heavier fabric, you might try multiplying it by 2.5. Then add an elastic waistband and a sassy red ribbon and you are done. Pack your bags for Greece and don't forget your Jackie O. sunglasses.

FINISHED SIZE

*Width: 12 1/2" (32cm) at waist;
38" (96.5cm) at hem*

Height: 25" (63.5cm), including trim

MATERIALS

Skirt: 2 1/2 yards ✱ *(2.3m) cotton or linen fabric*

Trim: 1 1/4 yards (1.1m) dark cotton fabric, or piece together enough for 2 pieces 5 1/2" deep (14cm) x the width of your skirt

3/4" (2cm) elastic the circumference of your waist

2 1/2 yards (2.3m) 3/8"- (19mm-) wide grosgrain ribbon

Bleach pen (see Resources, page 142)

Metal tip (for bleach pen)

Light chalk pencil for fabric

Sewing machine

✱ You will have to do some math to figure out the pattern pieces. If your waist is 28" (71cm) (an average medium), multiply by 3. That would be an 84"- (213cm-) wide piece of fabric, which will be cut into (2) 42"- (106.5cm-) wide pieces. Now measure your favorite skirt length from your closet. The knee-length skirt photographed is 23" (58.5cm) from waistband to hem (25" [63.5cm] before turning for waistband or hem). I cut 2 rectangles for the striped skirt part, each 42" wide x 25" deep (106.5 x 63.5cm), and 2 pieces for the bleached pen painted trim, each 42" wide x 5 1/2" deep (106.5 x 14cm).

STRIPED SKIRT CONTINUED

SEAM ALLOWANCE *¼" (6mm)*

TEMPLATE *page 140*

1 Read the Removing Dye with a Bleach Pen method (page 86). Cut out a piece from dark trim fabric 5½" (14cm) high by the same width as your skirt. Cut the piece in half to make 2 pieces, for the front and back. It might be necessary to piece the trim together to save fabric; sew pieces together to get as much as you need. Now hem one long edge on each piece by turning up one raw edge ¼" (6mm) twice, press, and topstitch. (I like to hem first for this project so I can see exactly how much drawing room I have with the bleach pen.)

2 Using a light chalk pencil, lightly draw a line onto the dark fabric, copying the template or using your own design. (Or don't bother tracing anything: Practice on a scrap first and then just go for it.)

3 Follow the line with your bleach pen fitted with the metal tip. Let sit for 30 minutes. Rinse with soapy water and let dry or iron dry. The line appears lighter when wet. **A**

4 Cut out the front and back skirt rectangles. Lay the bleached trim to the bottom front of the skirt, right sides together. Stitch and press the seams flat. Repeat with the skirt back. Stitch front and back skirt pieces together at the side, with right sides facing, making sure to align the trim at the side seams. Press the seams flat.

5 Make the casing for the elastic by turning ¼" (6mm) down on the top edge, and press. Turn again 1" (2.5cm) and stitch, leaving an opening to insert the elastic. Attach a safety pin to the end of the elastic and guide the elastic through the casing, using the safety pin as something to hold onto. Try the skirt on and adjust the elastic length if necessary. Overlap the elastic, stitch together, and sew the casing opening closed. **B**

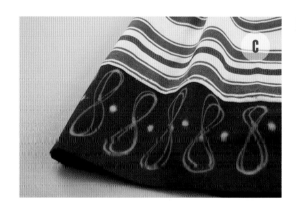

6 Stitch through the elastic from the top edge 1" (2.5cm) down at the side seams to keep it from twisting.

7 Stitch the grosgrain ribbon onto the skirt fabric 2" (3cm) from the top of the trim with a wide zigzag stitch. **C** Fold over the raw end of ribbon before stitching down at the end.

TIPS, HINTS, AND OTHER SUGGESTIONS

» If using a striped fabric, make sure it is running in the direction you want before you cut.

» Try using a bleach pen on existing clothes, especially items that you aren't attached to. You might love the result.

LACE NECKLACE

Dollmakers and folk artists have been dyeing laces and trims in teacups for ages. Tea or coffee adds a lovely worn look to the lace and gives it a sepia hue, making it perfect for a weathered project. These lace necklaces are an edgier version of this fun technique. Add a vintage button and a bit of Velcro®, and you have a choker that is both super cool and super easy.

• •

FINISHED SIZE

Blue necklace: 15¼" x ⅞" (39 x 2.2cm)

Orange necklace: 14½" x 1" (37 x 2.5cm)

MATERIALS

1¼ yards (1.1m) cotton lace in various widths from ½" to 1" (13–25mm) for several necklaces

Dye-Na-Flow textile paint in various colors

Velcro® strips

Decorative button

Craft glue (optional)

Sewing machine

1. Read the Painting with Dye method (page 83). Wrap the lace around your neck and mark where it's comfortable, adding 3" (7.5cm) for the hem. Cut the lace to this measurement.

2. Paint dye on both sides of the lace and let dry. Heat-set the dye with an iron. **A**

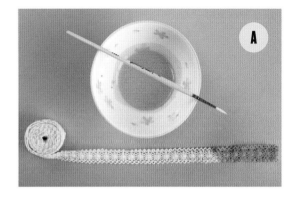

3. Cut Velcro® squares slightly narrower than the lace. Fold lace ends over ½" (13mm) and then again. Stitch Velcro to the folded edge with a straight stitch around all four sides of the square. You may have to trim the Velcro® piece to conceal it behind the lace. Make sure to place one side of the Velcro® on the inside of one end and the other side of the Velcro® on the outside of the other end. **B**

4. Hand-stitch a button to the middle of your necklace. If it sags, add a little bit of craft glue to keep it upright.

TIPS, HINTS, AND OTHER SUGGESTIONS

» It's fun to make several of these at once. Lay them all out assembly-line style. Cut shorter ones for bracelets.

» Try other trims. Felt flowers, other ribbons, and even small charms would be lovely.

» Hang beads from the lace by adding a jump ring and a bead suspended from the bottom edge. Just make sure it's not too heavy.

» The lace needs to be cotton to accept the dye. Hand wash your lace in the sink first to get rid of any sizing; sometimes it's hard for the dye to saturate if it's unwashed.

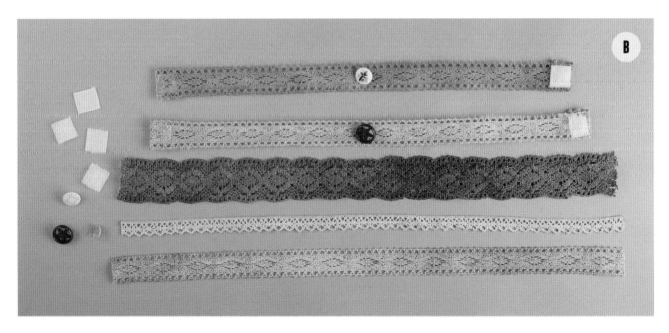

EMBELLISHED SWEATER

I find it almost impossible to wear cardigan sweaters without some sort of embellishment. A workhorse in most wardrobes, the classic cardigan is a prime candidate for some dressing up. Go to your existing sweaters first and listen closely. One of them will be saying "Choose me!" Time to make her extra pretty. Swap out the boring buttons, add some dyed lace and some over-dyed fabric leaves, and you are ready to go out. She will thank you, and you will feel like a genius.

● ●

MATERIALS

Cardigan sweater, either new or from your closet

1 yard (91cm) white lace in width of your choice (this sweater has ¹/₂" [13mm] lace)

Procion dye

Buttons to replace existing buttons (make sure they will fit the button-holes)

6" x 6" (15 x 15cm) scrap fabric for overdyeing appliqué embellishment

¹/₂ yard (45.5cm) ³/₈" (9mm) satin ribbon

HeatnBond Lite

Sewing machine

TEMPLATE *page 140*

1   Read the Basic Small-Quantity Dyeing method (page 81). Using Procion dye, dye the fabric and lace in a small plastic cup. **A**

2   Once your fabric and lace are dyed, rinsed, and dry, transfer leaf shapes (using template on page 140) to HeatnBond Lite. Apply to the back side of your overdyed fabric and sew onto your sweater. Read the HeatnBond instructions for application tips and sewing directions.

3   Press dyed lace with an iron, and, using a straight stitch, sew onto the front of the sweater, turning raw edges of lace under to the inside of the sweater at the top of the neck and the bottom of the hem. **B**

4   Replace the existing buttons with fancy new ones. Tie satin ribbon in a bow, trim ends, and hand-stitch it to the top of the leaves and through the knot, anchoring the bows. **C**

TIPS, HINTS, AND OTHER SUGGESTIONS

》 Whenever you do small-batch dyeing, try adding patterned fabric scraps to the dye bath. Overdyeing is a fun way to make fabric match without it looking too matchy.

》 Try an even quicker method of lace dyeing and overdyeing with the Painting with Dye method (page 83). This works well on small pieces of trim. I encourage you to try this with actual dye as well—it's a great beginning step to getting comfortable mixing dye powders yourself. This will help you gain the confidence to dye bigger pieces such as full yards of fabric.

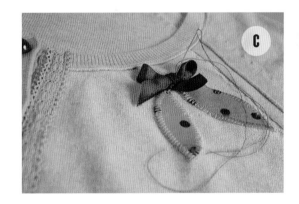

6

FIBER ON FABRIC

APPLY YARN, THREADS, AND OTHER
FABRICS TO YOUR PROJECTS TO GIVE
THEM A TOTALLY NEW LOOK.

★ ★

DRAWING WITH THREAD

Thread drawing on fabric, also called free-motion stitching or needle play, is one of my favorite techniques. Imagine grabbing a pencil and drawing on fabric any which way, but now imagine those lines as thread instead of lead. Of course, it's a bit harder moving fabric under a sewing machine foot than it is drawing with a pencil, but you'd be surprised how easy it becomes after a few practice sessions.

Most machines have the ability to do this stitch. You will need two things: a free-motion sewing (or darning) foot for your machine and the ability to lower your feed dogs (this is also done with a darning stitch, so your machine's manual may reference it that way). The free-motion foot looks like a normal foot with a little loop. This foot is a specialized one, so it may not come with your machine; buy it at a shop that sells your brand of machine, or have the shop order one for you.

Trying out this method on felt first is a big advantage. The felt stays stable and is easy to maneuver with your hands. After you get a feel for this, you can try it on thinner fabrics, usually with an iron-on stabilizer, like in I Drew on This!, page 112. You can even secure the fabric in a small embroidery hoop for a better grip while sewing.

1 Transfer the template or your design onto the felt using a pencil. Marking felt can be tricky; sometimes it's easier to just sew directly onto the felt and not follow any lines.

2 Refer to your sewing manual for how to lower your feed dogs and attach your free-motion sewing foot (or darning foot.) Once you have figured this out, lower the presser foot to start sewing. The foot won't touch your fabric, but that's okay. Now start sewing a line. *You* will have to move your fabric. Lowering the feed dogs means the machine won't move it for you, so hold the corners of the felt and move the fabric under the foot while you sew, keeping constant pressure on the foot pedal. Notice if you move the fabric fast, the stitch will be longer.

3 Play around—go up and down and side to side. Practice. Scribble and make a big mess. You'll notice that the lines look better when you retrace them over and over. A Vary your speed, motion, and the scale of your images. Now write your name.

4 When finishing (and starting), make tiny stitches to keep the thread

BASIC MATERIALS
10" x 12" (20.5 x 30.5cm) piece of wool felt to practice on

Pencil to mark felt (a standard #2 pencil works best)

6–8" (15-20.5cm) wooden embroidery hoop (optional)

Sewing machine with a darning foot or free-motion sewing foot

TEMPLATE *page 129*

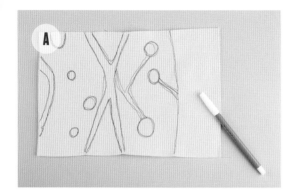

DRAWING WITH THREAD CONTINUED

from unraveling after you clip the ends. By tiny, I mean about 7–8 stitches per $\frac{1}{4}$" (6mm).

WHY THIS METHOD WILL MAKE YOU HAPPY:

★ This is a wonderful way to give an item a hand-stitched look without actually hand-stitching.

★ Can't draw? Don't try! This method looks better when it's sloppy.

WHY THIS METHOD MIGHT MAKE YOU SAD:

★ Some machines can free-motion stitch better than others. If you are struggling with your machine, inserting a new needle might help.

★ After working with felt, you might be frustrated when thread-drawing on other fabrics. Try using a lightweight iron-on interfacing on the back side of the fabric for stability.

TIPS, HINTS, AND OTHER SUGGESTIONS

>> If gripping and moving your fabric is driving you crazy, secure it in an embroidery hoop first. Make sure to secure the fabric tightly. You can use the hoop to grip the fabric when moving it around. It seems like the hoop won't fit under the foot, but it will—try it. Many sewers *only* free-motion with the fabric in a hoop, but I find the size constraint limiting. If I am working small, I use a hoop, but if I am stitching all over, I just move the fabric around with my hands.

>> Wearing gripper gloves, sold in quilt shops, will help you keep the sewing area taut. These are wonderful if your hands are too dry and the fabric is slipping.

COUCHING WITH THREAD AND YARN

Couching may be a funny-sounding word, but it's a very cool technique. You have probably done it before without knowing it had a name. Couching is when you lay thread or yarn across fabric and sew it in place with another thread, anchoring it down. Typically this is done with thread, but you can use almost any fiber. I love to do it with yarn. Often after finishing a knitting project, a little yarn is left, and usually it's too good not to reuse. This is a perfect project for those bits and pieces of saved yarn. Couching is usually done by hand, but sometimes I like to use a machine. The speed of the machine allows me to compose quickly and not overanalyze the random placement of the yarns. A clever trick is to use a light fabric spray adhesive to keep the yarn in place while laying it out and stitching—it works like a charm. A simple zigzag stitch across the yarn anchors it beautifully.

1   If your project will need to be laundered, prewash your yarn.

2   Lay out the fabric you will be stitching onto and lightly spray with the spray glue. Cut lengths of yarn and place them onto your fabric in the pattern you like, pressing down to keep in place. Simple shapes work best. Pin larger areas so they won't shift while you stitch. **A**

3   Using a zigzag stitch, sew over the yarn, following the direction of the design. Adjust the width of the zigzag stitch so it's wide enough to cover the yarn thickness. Continue sewing over all of the lines of the yarn, repositioning and pivoting the fabric as necessary. Try creating different lines and shapes with the yarn. **B**

MATERIALS

Fabric to stitch the yarn or thread to; any old fabric will do, or try an existing clothing item

Yarn in any weight you like, but for the most textural effect, go for bulky weight. One skein is more than you need. Try hitting up your knitting friends for leftover yarn if you don't have any yourself.

Sulky Spray KK 2000 Temporary Spray Adhesive

Straight pins

Sewing machine

COUCHING WITH THREAD AND YARN CONTINUED

WHY THIS METHOD WILL MAKE YOU HAPPY:

★ This is so fiber-arty cool I can't stand it. It's a great technique to add to existing clothes and bags, not to mention new sewing projects.

★ You can change the look of this with thinner yarn. Imagine a red worsted weight on cream fabric—very simple and lovely.

WHY THIS METHOD MIGHT MAKE YOU SAD:

★ Yarn frays, felts, and gets fuzzy. I dig this look, but if it will bug you, the smaller your zigzag stitches (in length, not width), the more attached the yarn will stay.

★ If trimming an existing project with this method, make sure your sewing machine needle can get to where your yarn/thread is laid out. Sounds obvious, but I have made this mistake before.

MAKING IRON-ON FABRIC PATCHES

These are easy and very fun to make. Using an adhesive-backed fusible web, make your favorite fabric into supercute patches. You will find yourself putting homemade patches on everything. You have to sew them on after you iron them in place, which means simple shapes are best—easy to cut out, and, more importantly, easy to machine-stitch. They are great for T-shirts, onesies, skirts, blankets, sweaters, hats, even patches on elbows and pants. Things to think about first: You'll need to iron this on before you sew, so the patch material needs to be able to accept heat. Also, the item will need to be able to fit in your sewing machine. I am embarrassed to admit I have ironed on patches only to realize I can't reach the patch with my sewing machine needle. Oops! Don't do what I did. If this happens to you, remember you can always hand-stitch it; it's just a little more time-consuming and possibly not as secure.

1 Prewash and dry your patch fabric if it will need to be laundered.

2 Transfer your design to the paper side of the HeatnBond Lite adhesive with a pencil. Cut out a piece of your patch fabric larger than your design. Iron the adhesive onto the wrong side of your fabric according to the manufacturer's instructions.

3 Let the patch cool, and with good, sharp sewing scissors, cut out your shape right on the line you drew, cutting through both the paper backing and the fabric. Now remove the paper backing, exposing the thin layer of glue fused to the fabric. **A**

4 Position this patch, glue side down, onto your T-shirt or fabric (again, referring to the manufacturer's instructions). Press. Using a small zigzag stitch, machine-stitch around the shape, backstitching to anchor the threads when you are done (otherwise it may come off after several washings). **B**

WHY THIS METHOD WILL MAKE YOU HAPPY:

★ Lots of bang for your buck! It's very inexpensive and very rewarding.

★ This can be used for multiples; you can stack and cut several shapes at a time.

★ This method works on both existing clothes and raw fabric. For a quilt, try this method instead of traditional appliqué.

WHY THIS METHOD MIGHT MAKE YOU SAD:

★ The patches need to be simple shapes—think circles and squares.

★ A large patch will change the way fabric drapes, making it unsuitable for very lightweight fabrics.

TIPS, HINTS, AND OTHER SUGGESTIONS

≫ For a perfect-looking zigzag finish, don't backstitch at the end. Instead leave a long tail on the last stitch and thread a needle with the tail, stitch through to the back, and secure with a knot on the back side. Backstitching a zigzag can look messy, especially on a circle. Having said that, I often just backstitch anyway and don't worry about it. Only you know if it will bug you or not.

MATERIALS

Clothing or item to sew patches onto

Fabric for your patches (quilting cotton is perfect)

Adhesive backed fusible web such as HeatnBond Lite

Sewing machine

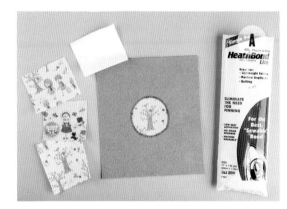

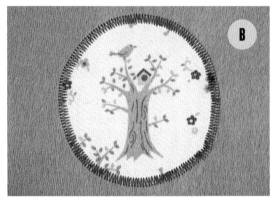

DRAWN BOOKCOVER

Spice up your favorite sketchbook with this easy-to-make felt cover. You can leave the felt plain or add this naughty little drawing using the Drawing with Thread method. This cover fits a standard Moleskine sketchbook and uses one standard-sized piece of felt. How easy is that?

FINISHED SIZE
7³/₄" total width x 5³/₄" high (19.5 x 14.5cm); flaps are 2" wide (5cm)

MATERIALS
1 sheet felt, 8¹/₂" x 12" (21.5 x 30.5cm) or larger (wool felt strongly recommended; see Resources, page 142)

Moleskine sketchbook or similar hard-bound sketchbook, 3¹/₂" x 5¹/₂" x ³/₄" (9 x 14 x 2cm)

Water-soluble or vanishing pen

TEMPLATE *page 140*

1   Read the Drawing with Thread method (page 103). Lay the sketchbook flat on the felt, cover side down. Trace the top and bottom of the book, extending the lines across the entire length of felt (the extra width on the sides, when folded over, will create flaps to tuck the sketchbook into). Add ¼" (6mm) above and below your marked line, and cut the lower piece out of the felt. You will trim the extra ¼" (6mm) off later, after you stitch.

2   Center the sketchbook flat on the felt, cover side down, and mark where the front cover will be positioned. Transfer the template design to the felt with a water-soluble pen. **A**

3   Free-motion stitch the design on the felt, following the template.

4   With the wrong side of the cover facing up, fold the extra 2" (5cm) over on both ends and pin. Stitch across the top and bottom, on top of the marked lines, sewing over the flaps as you stitch across. Trim the extra felt on the top and bottom to ⅛" (3mm) from the stitching line. Spray away the water-soluble pen lines with water. **B**

TIPS, HINTS, AND OTHER SUGGESTIONS

»   Wool felt is a dream to work with—it has a better feel and offers a richer selection of colors than acrylic craft felt. It's worth seeking out and using instead. It comes in other sizes, too (see Resources, page 142), so you can cover any size notebook.

»   It's often easier to draw directly with the thread rather than trying to follow a traced design. Use the markings as a guide only, and don't worry about going off the lines. The messy look works best here.

MY KID DREW ON THIS!

If you want to see a kid light up, give her a pen and a T-shirt and tell her to draw on it. She will look at you like you are crazy and then have the time of her life. This easy project requires nothing more than a kid, a sewing machine, and a water-soluble or vanishing pen. Tell the kid to draw simple shapes and not to color in, or her quick project might take longer than she thought. Now all you need to do is follow the lines with the Drawing with Thread method.

MATERIALS

T-shirt, dress, tank top, or another clothing item to draw onto ✱

Chalk pencil

Lightweight fusible interfacing if using a knit fabric, like a T-shirt

Embroidery hoop (optional)

Sewing machine with a darning foot or free-motion sewing foot

✱ *For this project I used a blank cotton jersey dress (see Resources, page 142). I dyed it pink first, and then I drew on it with thread.*

1   Read the Drawing with Thread method (page 103). If you are using a ready-to-dye garment, dye it first using the Basic Small-Quantity Dyeing method (page 80). If not, get out your T-shirt, tank top, or whatever you are using and find your kid. **A**

2   Tell your kid to draw on the garment. Try to limit the drawing time to about 10 minutes. Try a chalk fabric pencil, since heat-setting may make water-soluble ink permanent. You might have to edit out some of the drawing if the design or its location makes it challenging to sew.

3   Cut out a piece of interfacing slightly larger than the size of the drawing. Make sure your fabric is nice and smooth before fusing the interfacing to the fabric. Turn the garment inside out and press the interfacing directly behind the drawn-on areas. This will keep knit fabric from puckering when you stitch. Fusible interfacing can melt easily, so read the manufacturer's instructions. **B**

4   Stitch, using the Drawing with Thread method. You can use an embroidery hoop to secure the fabric while stitching, but only if your drawing fits within the hoop's circumference; otherwise, you will have to stop, reposition your fabric in the hoop, and start again. This will drive you batty, so if your drawing is large, skip the hoop and just move the fabric with your hands. **C**

TIPS, HINTS, AND OTHER SUGGESTIONS

》 This method looks best if you trace over the drawn lines several times with the thread. A scratchy style looks better than trying to make a perfect line.

I DREW ON THIS!

Don't relegate doodling to your sketchbook—transfer some of your great drawings to your shirt. This method lends itself to a messy, stretchy style, and you will love how it transforms the most basic shirt, skirt, or bag into something special. Using the same method as My Kid Drew on This! (page 110), you can now have a cool shirt, too. 'Cause you're still a kid, right?

MATERIALS

T-shirt, dress, tank top, or another clothing item to draw onto

Water-soluble or vanishing pen or, for dark fabrics, chalk pencil

Lightweight fusible interfacing for knits

Embroidery hoop (optional)

Sewing machine with a darning foot or free-motion sewing foot

TEMPLATE *page 141*

1 Read the Drawing with Thread method (page 103). Transfer the template or draw directly on your clothing with a water-soluble pen or vanishing pen. For dark fabrics, use a chalk fabric pencil.

2 Using the drawing sizes as a guide, cut out a piece of interfacing slightly larger than the size of the drawing. Make sure your fabric is nice and smooth before fusing the interfacing to the fabric. Turn the garment inside out and press the interfacing directly behind the drawn-on areas. Completely cover the reverse side of the drawing with the interfacing. This will keep the knit from puckering when you stitch. Fusible interfacing can melt easily, so read the manufacturer's instructions. **A**

3 Stitch, using the Drawing with Thread method. You can use an embroidery hoop to secure the fabric while stitching, but only if your drawing fits within the hoop's circumference; otherwise, you will have to stop, reposition your fabric in the hoop, and start again. This will drive you batty, so if your drawing is large, skip the hoop and just move the fabric with your hands. **B**

TIPS, HINTS, AND OTHER SUGGESTIONS

» The larger the area of thread drawing, the more the hand of the garment will change. Some puckering and shifting is part of the look, but if this bugs you, keep your drawing confined to a small area.

» The fusible interfacing will change the drape of clothes—not much, but you will be able to tell, so tissue-weight T-shirts are not recommended for this method. Stick to knits in normal T-shirt weight or heavier.

YARNY HANDBAG

This bag is haute! Combining a fiber-arty yarn with fun clear acrylic handles makes this chic little bag an awesome accessory. It's a simple bag to sew—you make it extra special by stitching yarn right onto the surface. The handles are easily tied on with extra yarn. So cool and fun, with such little effort.

FINISHED SIZE
11¹/₂" wide x 9" tall (29 x 23cm)

MATERIALS
*¹/₃ yard (30.5cm) outer bag fabric
(I used a mini corduroy): (2) 10" x 13"
(25.5 x 33cm) pieces*

*¹/₃ yard (30.5cm) lining fabric (I used
a canvas-weight cotton): (2) 10" x 13"
(25.5 x 33cm) pieces*

*1 skein hand-dyed nubby yarn or thick
yarn of your choice. I used a thick
and thin handspun yarn called Maisy
Day Handspun Merino wool yarn in
Tropicana (6) (see Resources,
page 142)*

   *(25) 13" (33cm) strands (depending
   on yarn thickness) for bag design*

   (4) 4" (10cm) strands for handle ties

*Clear acrylic handbag handles (see
Resources, page 142)*

Water-soluble pen or chalk pencil

*Sulky Spray KK 2000 Temporary
Spray Adhesive*

Sewing machine

1 Read the Couching with Thread and Yarn method (page 105). Cut out the pattern pieces and yarn strands. Using a chalk pencil or water-soluble pen, starting ¹/₄" (6mm) from the edge, draw lines on the fabric 1" (2.5cm) apart. These will be your stitching lines. You can eyeball these; they don't have to be precise.

2 Spray the 2 outer fabric pieces with Sulky Spray. Lay out the yarn strands about ³/₄" (2cm) apart, depending on your yarn size. These will run perpendicular to your stitching lines. You may not use all of the strands. Press firmly. **A**

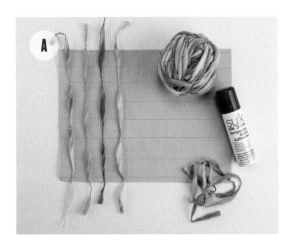

3 Following your marked stitching lines, stitch across the yarn. Trim off extra yarn. **B**

4 With right sides together, sew the sides and across the bottom of the lining fabric. Flare the corner out and mark ½" (13cm) from the corner up the side seam to make the box bottom. Stitch across the marked line. Trim the excess. Repeat on the other corner. **C**

5 Place the outer bag pieces right sides together and repeat step 4. You now have 2 bags—1 in the lining fabric, 1 in the outer bag fabric—with box bottoms.

6 Turn the outer bag wrong side out, then place the lining bag inside, right sides together. Stitch around the top, leaving an opening for turning. Turn right side out and press. Center handles on the bag and mark through the holes where the handle ties will be attached.

7 Pin the handle ties to the markings and topstitch around the top edge of the bag, catching the opening closed and sewing over the ties. Thread the handle ties through the handle openings and tie in a double knot. Trim the ties, or don't, if you like the look of them long. **D**

TIPS, HINTS, AND OTHER SUGGESTIONS

» Changing the type of yarn will change the look of this bag. For a more natural look, try neutral colors.

» A different way to couch the yarn is by simply zigzagging over it. This is easier and quicker but means you won't have any horizontal stripes as a design element.

» Yarn applied in this way will start to felt and fuzz after a bit of wear. I like the fuzzy look of frayed yarn, but if this bag will see heavy use, you might want to zigzag stitch over the yarn to keep it from fraying.

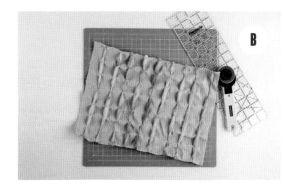

I HEART FABRIC PATCHES

Get that plain T-shirt out of your closet and make it your own. You can make these iron-on patches in any simple shape, but I particularly love to use hearts. They're great for using up scraps of fabric, but you could make pajama pants in fabric matching the patch. Super cute!

FINISHED SIZE

Large heart: 5¼" wide x 3½" high in the center (13 x 9cm)

Small heart: 2⅝" wide x 1¾" high in the center (6.5 x 4.5cm)

MATERIALS

T-shirt

Large heart patch fabric: (1) 6" x 7" (15 x 18cm) piece

Small heart patch fabric: (1) 3½" x 3" (9 x 7.5cm) piece

Adhesive-backed fusible web such as HeatnBond Lite

Sewing machine

PATTERN *page 141*

1 Read the Making Iron-On Fabric Patches method (page 106). Using the template, trace the heart shapes onto the paper side of the fusible web. **A**

2 Iron fusible web onto the patch fabric. Let cool, and trim on the traced line marking the heart shape. Peel off the paper backing and press to the T-shirt. Stitch to the T-shirt when cool, using a small zigzag stitch over the edge of the heart.

3 Repeat steps 1 and 2 with the small inner heart. **B**

TIPS, HINTS, AND OTHER SUGGESTIONS

>> These are cute for jeans, bags, and whatever you want to embellish. Just remember that you'll be stitching around the shape on a sewing machine, so keep the shapes simple.

CUSTOM BABY SHIRT

This is one of my all time favorite projects. Perfect for gifts for other babies as well as your own, you will be making these like crazy. The same method as in I Heart Fabric Patches (page 116) is used, but these mini versions are extra fun because you get to use all of the sweet little kid fabric that you wouldn't use on your own clothes. (Or maybe you would!) Keep your scraps around, because this project is perfect for them.

1 Read the Making Iron-On Fabric Patches method (page 106). Cut out a simple rectangle of your favorite cute fabric. A 3¼" x 3½" (8.25 x 9cm) size is good for baby clothes. **A**

2 Iron fusible web to the patch fabric. Let cool, and trim away excess. Peel off the paper backing and press onto the T-shirt. Stitch down when cool, using a small zigzag stitch over the edge of the rectangle. **B**

TIPS, HINTS, AND OTHER SUGGESTIONS

» Buy a 3-pack of baby T-shirts or onesies so you have some on hand when you need a quick gift.

» If you are making a baby quilt or other item, use the scraps from that project to make patches for a matching baby T-shirt.

» Older kids love to be able to customize their own clothes. Lay out a bunch of fabric scraps and let them design their own patches. Just make sure the shapes stay simple, so you can stitch around them. This is a great first sewing project for kids, and it's instant gratification!

» Ditch the goodie bags at a kids' party. Instead, have them bring their own shirt to decorate! Lay out scraps beforehand (providing simple shapes to trace if needed, like circles and squares; lids and boxes work well as templates) and have an adult iron and sew. With all of the great fabrics out there now, finding designs for both genders is really easy.

FINISHED SIZE
3¼" wide x 3½" tall (8.25 x 9cm) patch

MATERIALS
Baby lap T-shirt or onesie

Patch fabric: (1) 3¼" x 3½" (8.25 x 9cm) piece (or whatever size works with your design)

Adhesive-backed fusible web such as HeatnBond Lite

Sewing machine

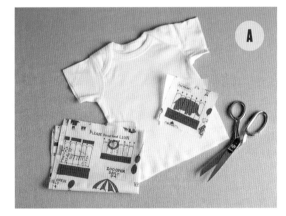

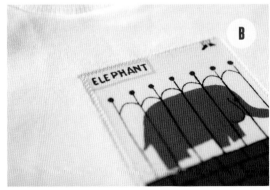

TEMPLATES AND PATTERNS

Make a copy of the template or the pattern at the magnification percentage listed for each, and trace onto your fabric. Or, if you are using white fabric, and if the template is included at 100 percent, try laying the fabric right over the page in the book. Instead of using a fabric marking pen or pencil, you could try a nonwaxy paper to trace designs directly onto your fabric. For easy tracing, tape the copy on a window and then tape your fabric over that. If it's nighttime, you can tape onto a (turned-on) television or computer screen and get the same effect.

To transfer designs from this section and from your own sketchbook, use water-soluble pens, chalk pencils, vanishing pens, or transfer pencils (used with an iron and tracing paper, or used directly on your fabric). Chalk pencils work well on dark fabrics; the marks wash out easily. Some water-soluble pens set permanently with heat, so if you need to heat-set, use a transfer pencil, vanishing pen, or another transfer method.

Some projects need to be copied onto fabric sheets. You can do this in two ways: Scan the template and print it directly onto your fabric from your printer, or take the template to a copy shop and copy it onto a fabric sheet on a color copier. Fabric sheets are made specifically for color copiers, so check and make sure you have the right ones (see Resources, page 142). Some templates in this book are available online as PDFs in full color, so you won't have to go to the copy shop at all. All you have to do is enter the password (FABRICPLAY), download the PDF, then print it onto your fabric sheets at home. How clever! Go to amykarol.com for the templates.

Please note: There are rules about what copy shops can copy for you, especially when what you want to copy comes from a book. In small quantities, for personal use, you are free to make photocopies from this book, but some copy shops may not allow you to photocopy other copyrighted materials.

CARVING YOUR OWN STAMPS 33

USE AT 100%

STAMPING WITH FOAM 34

USE AT 100%

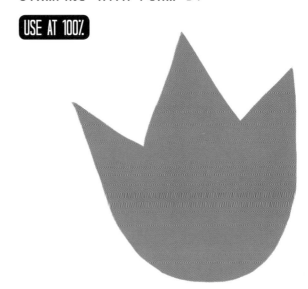

FREEHAND PAINTING WITH A BRUSH 30

USE AT 100%

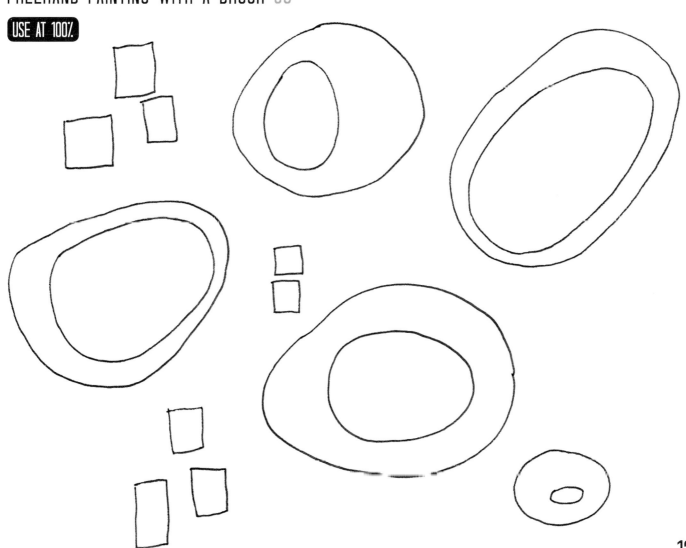

DRAWING WITH PAINT AND A METAL TIP 36

USE AT 200%

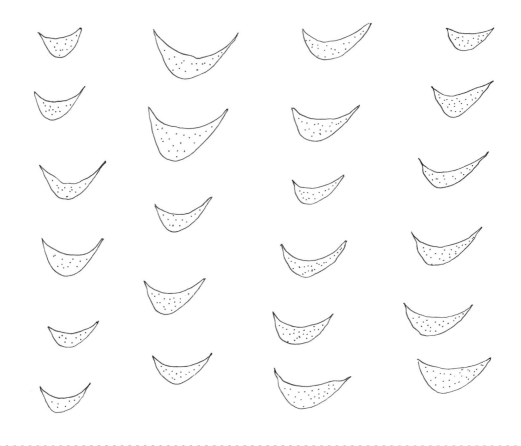

USE AT 200%

REMOVING DYE WITH A BLEACH PEN 87

USE AT 140%

REMOVING DYE WITH A BLEACH PEN 87

USE AT 170%

PRINTING IMAGES ONTO FABRIC SHEETS 54

USE AT 110%

APPLYING IRON-ON TRANSFERS 58

USE AT 125%.

AUNT SARAH AND UNCLE PETE DOLLS 62

Also available online at www.amykarol.com

USE AT 110%.

APPLYING OPAQUE IRON-ON TRANSFERS 59
Also available online at www.amykarol.com

USE AT 100%.

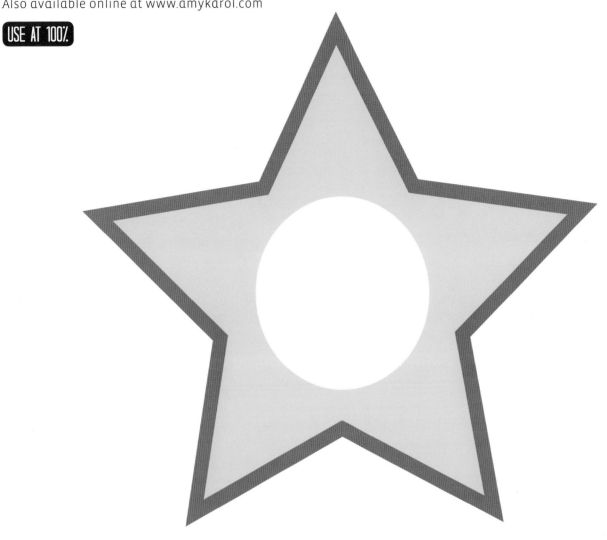

STAMPED BELT 42

USE AT 100%.

CREATING YOUR OWN FABRIC SHEETS (OPPOSITE) 56

USE AT 100%.

DRAWING WITH THREAD 103

`USE AT 170%`

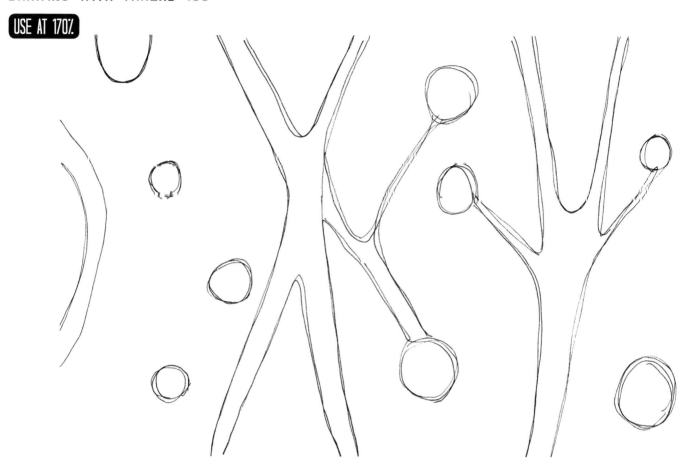

SCREEN PRINTING WITH PHOTOEZ 60

`USE AT 180%`

A WORD ABOUT NOTETAKING 23

USE AT 100%

PROJECT NAME

DATE

MATERIALS USED

FABRIC SWATCH

WHAT I LOVE ABOUT IT

WHAT'S NOT QUITE RIGHT

NOTES/REMINDERS

IF MY TOTES COULD SPEAK 68
Also available online at www.amykarol.com

loose

change

keys

of none

your

business

might be

garbage

BAND T-SHIRTS! 75

USE AT 100%

THE

it's not my bedtime

FAMILY BAND

YOUR BLOUSE, ONLY COOLER 40

USE AT 100%

ONE-OF-A-KIND CLUTCH (BELOW AND ON FOLLOWING PAGE) 48

USE BELOW AT 100% AND ON FOLLOWING PAGE AT 105%

BABY PILLOW (BELOW AND ON FOLLOWING PAGE) 70

Template also available online at www.amykarol.com

USE AT 100%

WATERCOLOR TOTE (PREVIOUS PAGE) 72

USE AT 105%.

WATERCOLOR TOTE STRAP END 72

USE AT 100%.

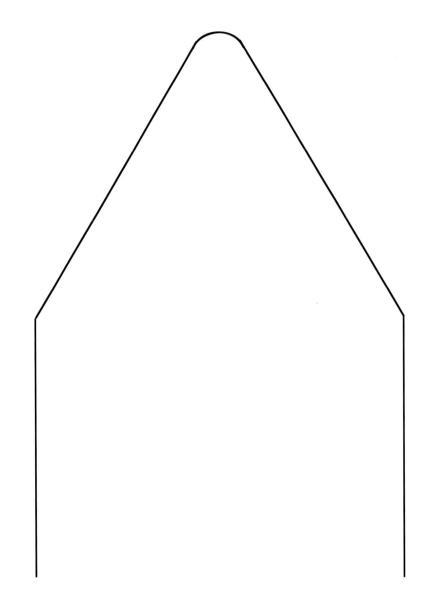

MODERN BEDSHEETS 76

USE AT 120%.

SOFT ART: WHOLE-CLOTH QUILT 93

USE AT 100%: YOU MAY WANT TO ENLARGE A FEW TO MIX UP THE DESIGN

STRIPED SKIRT 97

`USE AT 100%`

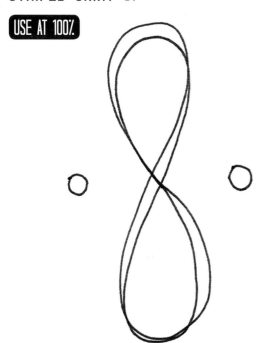

EMBELLISHED SWEATER 100

`USE AT 100%`

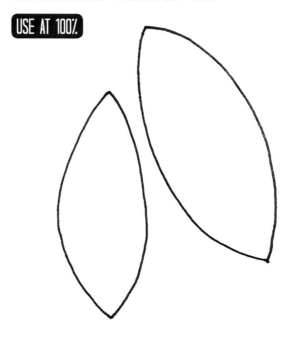

DRAWN BOOKCOVER 108

`USE AT 100%`

I DREW ON THIS! 112

USE AT 100%.

I HEART FABRIC PATCHES 116

USE AT 100%.

RESOURCES

Many supplies used in these projects can be found at your local craft shop or fabric store. Shop locally first—I love supporting shops in my neighborhood and hope you can do the same. I also greatly appreciate the Internet and love being able to shop 24 hours a day, so here's a list for you. It's not exhaustive, so feel free to shop around and compare prices.

ACRYLIC MOUNTING BLOCKS AND RUBBER STAMP INKS FOR FABRICS

Blockheads Paper Arts
www.blockheadstamps.com
sr@www.blockheadstamps.com

COTTON CANVAS STRAPPING

TwillTape.com
www.twilltape.com
800-876-4783

CRAFT PUNCHES

Martha Stewart Crafts
www.marthastewartcrafts.com
877-882-0319

FABRIC DYES. TEXTILE PAINTS. IRON-ON TRANSFERS. BLANK. READY-TO-DYE FABRIC AND CLOTHING. BUBBLE JET SET 2000. FABRIC MARKERS AND PENS. BOTTLES AND PAINT APPLICATORS. FREEZER PAPER. FOAM FOR STAMPING. WATER-BASED RESISTS. AND JUST ABOUT EVERYTHING ELSE YOU NEED

Dharma Trading Co
www.dharmatrading.com
800-542-5227

HANDBAG HANDLES AND BELT BUCKLES

M&J Trimming
www.mjtrim.com
800-9-MJTRIM

HAND-DYED YARN

Hello Yarn
www.helloyarn.com
yarn@helloyarn.com

HEATNBOND LITE AND VARIOUS IRON-ON INTERFACINGS. RIBBONS. BUTTONS. AND SEWING NOTIONS

Jo-Ann Fabric and Craft Stores
www.joann.com
888-739-4120

MOLESKINE SKETCHBOOKS

Moleskine
www.moleskine.com
info@moleskine.com

PHOTOEZ SCREEN-PRINTING KITS

EZScreenPrint
www.ezscreenprint.com
520-423-0409

RUBBER STAMPS

The Small Object
www.thesmallobject.com
info@thesmallobject.com

STAMP CARVING BLOCKS, CARVING TOOLS, BRUSHES, AND GENERAL ART SUPPLIES

Blick Art Materials
www.dickblick.com
800-828-4548

SULKY KK 2000™ TEMPORARY SPRAY ADHESIVE

Sulky
www.sulky.com
800-874-4115

TEXTILE PAINTS, IRON-ON TRANSFERS, READY-TO-DYE FABRIC AND CLOTHING, FABRIC MARKERS AND PENS, BOTTLES AND PAINT APPLICATORS, FREEZER PAPER, FOAM FOR STAMPING

Michaels
www.michaels.com
800-MICHAELS

WOOL FELT

Weir Dolls & Crafts
www.weirdolls.com
734-668-6992

ACKNOWLEDGMENTS

I have to pinch myself every time I look at this book. The amazing team of talent at Potter Craft has done it again; Rosy Ngo, Amy Sly, Courtney Conroy, Jen Graham, Thom O'Hearn— you all rock the house. For real. I was thrilled to work with the mighty talented Alexandra Grablewski (photographer) and Leslie Siebel (stylist) once again. I think lightning struck twice. Big thanks and a bear hug to photographer Matt Wong, who provided the step-by-step photos. Thanks to Grammie for her eagle eye, help with the girls, and moral support, and to Mariko Fujinaka, my crafter/editor all-star. Sarah Sockit, thank you again for being you, and big love to my family, friends, and cohorts: I couldn't do this without you.

INDEX